THE EPISTLE OF JAMES

William MacDonald

Original text material by William MacDonald
Developed as a correspondence course by
Emmaus Correspondence School

ISBN 0-940293-35-8

789/098

INSTRUCTIONS TO STUDENTS

We designed this material to serve as a guided self-study correspondence course for your personal enrichment. You may use it that way or as a guide for a group Bible study. There are several different groups of people who take these courses. Please follow the instructions for your group.

INMATES IN CORRECTIONAL INSTITUTIONS

This book will contain one of the following ways for sending us your answers. Please pick the one that applies to you.

A. When exams are bound in the book or are separate from the book and there is no separate answer sheet, remove the exams from the book after you take all the exams. Send them to the people who sent the course to you.

B. When you receive a separate one-page answer sheet, write your answers on the sheet. Please return it to the people who sent you the course.

C. When the exam questions are separate from the book, and you have a one-page answer sheet, send only the one-page answer sheet to those who sent you the course.

INDIVIDUALS USING THE COURSES FOR THEIR OWN STUDY

A. Cost

When you purchased this course, the price did not include grading. We would encourage you to take advantage of the personal help you will receive by taking it as a correspondence course.

Send $2.00, along with the name of the course, and your name and address, to the address on the back cover. (If you received the course from an Emmaus representative, send the money and information to them.) You will receive an educational package, including a single page answer sheet, that will enroll you in the Emmaus Correspondence School.

B. Taking the Exams

As you study the material, you will come to exams on various sections of the book. Take each exam as it comes up recording your answers. When you have taken all the exams, transfer your answers to the single page answer sheet and return it for grading.

You will receive a credit certificate if your average grade is 70% or higher. If your average grade is less than 70%, you will receive a completion card.

C. Other Services

Emmaus offers about 60 books of Bible study presenting Salvation, New Testament Book Studies, and Topical Studies. These books are available to you from the office in Dubuque (see address on back cover). If you would like the convenience of service closer to home, let us know. We will send you the name of an Emmaus Associate Instructor in your area.

ABOUT THE EPISTLE OF JAMES

"Faith on trial" is the theme of this letter. Within its five short chapters, James puts our faith to the test. He wants to know if it is genuine or a cheap imitation.

"The letter speaks to us where we are," says D. A. Hayes, "in language we can understand. Its short sentences go like shots straight to the mark. We feel the impact and the impress of them. There is an energy behind them and a reality in them that makes them live in our thoughts."

This letter is strangely silent concerning the great fundamental doctrines of the Christian faith. for instance, neither the incarnation nor the resurrection are mentioned. In fact, the Name of Christ is found only twice (1:1 and 2:1).

But this is not so strange after all. The writer's purpose was not to teach doctrine so much as to show us how the Word should become incarnate in our lives, how we should manifest the life of the risen Christ to those about us. This he has done exceedingly well.

We trust you will enyoy this study and that the Holy Spirit will be able to accomplish in your life the goals He had in mind when He caused it to be written.

HOW TO STUDY

Begin by asking God to open your heart to receive the truths He would teach you from His Word. Read the lesson through at least twice, once to get the general drift of its contents and then again, slowly, looking up all Scripture references and examining all footnotes.

BIBLE VERSION

You may use any version of the Bible for general study. If you choose to take this as a correspondence course, however, please restrict yourself to either the Authorized (King James) Version (1611), or the New American Standard Version (1960), when answering exam questions. These are widely used versions. There are so many versions today that your instructor cannot possible check them all in evaluating your work.

THOUGHT AND RESEARCH QUESTIONS

Some exams contain questions designed to make you do original Bible study. You may use your Bible to answer these questions. They are clearly marked.

WHAT DO YOU SAY? QUESTIONS

Questions headed in this way are optional and no point value is assigned to them. You may freely state your own opinions in answer to such questions. Your candid answers will help your instructor get to know you better as an individual. They will also help us evaluate the general effectiveness of this course.

HOW YOUR PAPERS ARE GRADED

Any incorrectly answered questions will be marked by your instructor. You will be referred back to the place in the Bible or the textbook where the correct answer is to be found.

OUTLINE

Lesson 1

Trials and Temptations (James 1:1-17)

INTRODUCTION

To achieve his goal, James draws heavily on the teachings of the Lord Jesus in the Sermon on the Mount. This will be readily seen by the following comparison—

James	Parallel in Matthew	Subject
1:2, 12; 5:10	5:10-12	Adversity
1:5; 4:3; 5:13-18	6:6-13; 7:7-12	Prayer
1:8; 4:8	6:22, 23	The Single Eye
1:10, 11; 2:6, 7	6:19-21, 24-34	Wealth
1:19, 20; 4:1	5:22	Wrath
1:25; 2:1, 12, 13	5:17-44	The Law
1:26, 27	6:1-18	Mere Profession
2:8	7:12	The Royal Law
2:13	5:7	Mercy
2:14-26	7:15-27	Faith and Works
3:11, 12	7:16-20	Root and Fruit
3:13	7:24	True Wisdom
3:17, 18	5:9	The Peacemaker
4:11, 12	7:1-5	Judging Others
5:2	6:19	Rusted Treasures
5:12	5:33-37	Oaths

There are frequent references to the law in this letter. It is called "the perfect law" (1:25), "the royal law" (2:8) and "the law of liberty" (2:12). James does not teach that his readers are under law for salvation or as a rule of life. Rather, portions of the law are cited as instruction in righteousness for those who are under grace.

There are many resemblances to the book of Proverbs in James' letter. Like Proverbs, his style is rugged, vivid, graphic, and difficult to outline. The word *wisdom* recurs frequently.

Another key word in James is *brethren*. It occurs fifteen times, and reminds us that James is writing to believers, even if at times he seems to address the unconverted also.

In some ways, the letter of James is the most authoritarian in the New Testament. That is, James issues instructions more profusely than any of the other writers. In the short space of 108 verses, there are 54 imperatives.

THE GREETING (1:1)

The writer introduces himself as "James, a servant of God and of the Lord Jesus Christ." Which James is this? Several are mentioned in the New Testament. We cannot be absolutely sure which one wrote this letter. Most evangelical Christians assume it was James, the Lord's brother (Matthew 13:55; Mark 6:3), but we cannot be certain. We can be glad that this in no way affects the inspiration of the letter, or the benefit we can get from it.

If the author was the Lord's brother, as we suppose, then a wonderful change had come in his life. At one time, he had not believed in the Lord Jesus (John 7:5). He may have shared the prevalent view that Jesus was out of His mind (Mark 3:21). But our Lord patiently sowed the seed of the Word. Though unappreciated, He taught the great principles of the Kingdom of God. Then the seed took root in the life of James. A mighty transformation resulted. The skeptic became a servant. And he wasn't ashamed to say so!

He speaks of himself as a servant of God and of the Lord Jesus Christ, correctly putting God and the Lord Jesus on the same level as

2

equals. He honors the Son even as he honors the Father (John 5:23). James knew that "no man can serve two masters" (Matthew 6:24). Yet he spoke of himself as a servant of God and of the Lord Jesus. There is no contradiction here because God the Father and God the Son are co-equal.

The letter is addressed to the "twelve tribes which are scattered abroad," or "which are of the Dispersion" (RV). These people were Jews by birth, belonging to the twelve tribes of Israel. Because of Israel's sin, the people had been driven from their native land and were now dispersed in the countries surrounding the Mediterranean. The original dispersion took place when the ten tribes were carried into captivity by the Assyrians, 721 B.C., and when the other tribes were taken captive by the Babylonians, 586 B.C. Some of these returned to the land in the days of Ezra and Nehemiah, but only a remnant. On the day of Pentecost, devout Jews had visited Jerusalem from every nation of the then-known world (Acts 2:5). These could properly be called Jews of the Dispersion. But a later dispersion of Christian Jews took place. In Acts 8:1, we read that the early Christians (mostly of Jewish ancestry) were scattered abroad throughout Judea and Samaria by the persecutions of Saul. This dispersion is referred to again where we read that believers were driven to Phenice (Phoenicia), Cyprus and Antioch. Therefore, the people to whom James wrote could have been Jews who had been dispersed in any one of these crisis times.

Since all true believers are strangers and pilgrims in this world (Philippians 3:20; 1 Peter 2:11), we can apply this letter to ourselves, even if it wasn't written directly to us.

A more difficult question is whether James is addressing non-Christian Jews, Jews who had been converted to Christ, or both believing and unbelieving Jews. Primarily the author seems to be writing to true born again believers (1:18). Yet there are times when he seems to be addressing professing Christians or even the unconverted.

TRIALS AND TEMPTATIONS (1:2-17)

In this section James deals with the subject of temptation. He uses the word in two different senses. In verses 2-12, the temptations are what we might call holy trials or problems which are sent from God, and which test the reality of our faith and produce likeness to Christ. In verses 13-17, on the other hand, the subject is unholy temptations, which come from within, and which lead to sin.

1. Holy Trials (1:2-12)

The Christian life is filled with problems. They come uninvited and unexpected. Sometimes they come singly and sometimes in droves. They are inevitable. James does not say *"if* you fall into temptations" but *"when. . . ."* We can never get away from them. The question is "What are we going to do about them?"

There are several possible attitudes we can take toward the testings and trials of life. We can rebel against them (Hebrews 12:5) by adopting a spirit of defiance, boasting that we will battle through to victory by our own power. On the other hand, we can faint or give up under the pressure (Hebrews 12:5). We say, "What's the use? What's going to be is going to be." This is nothing but fatalism. It leads us to question even the Lord's care for us. We can grumble and complain about our troubles. This is what Paul warns us against in 1 Corinthians 10:10. We can indulge in self-pity, thinking of no one but ourselves, and trying to get sympathy from others. Or we can be exercised by the difficulties and perplexities of life (Hebrews 12:11). We can say, in effect, "God has allowed this trial to come to me. He has some good purpose in it for me. I don't know what that purpose is, but I'll try to find out. I want His purposes to be worked out in my life." This is what James advocates. "My brethren, count it all joy when ye fall into divers temptations." Don't rebel! Don't faint! Rejoice! These problems are not enemies, bent on destroying you. They are friends come to aid you in the development of Christian character.

God is trying to produce likeness to Christ in each of His children. This process necessarily involves suffering, frustration and perplexity. The fruit of the Spirit cannot be produced when

4

all is sunshine; there must be rain and dark clouds. Trials never seem pleasant; they seem very difficult and disagreeable. But afterwards they yield the peaceable fruit of righteousness to those who are exercised by them (Hebrews 12:11). How often we hear a Christian say, after passing through some great crisis, "It wasn't easy to take, but I wouldn't give up the experience for anything."

James speaks of "the trying of your faith" (verse 3). He pictures faith as a precious metal which is being tried by the Assayer (God) to see if it is genuine. The metal is subjected to the fires of persecution, sickness, suffering or sorrow.

James reminds us that the proving of our faith works "patience." A better word for patience here would be steadfastness or fortitude. As our faith is put to the test, we become strengthened to meet problems still to come. We may liken the process to a tree that is exposed to the winter gales. The pressure of the gales causes the roots to go down deeper and the tree itself becomes stronger. Without problems, we would never develop endurance. Even men of the world realize that problems strengthen character. Charles Kettering, noted industrialist once said, "Problems are the price of progress. Don't bring me anything but problems. Good news weakens me."

"But let patience have her perfect work . . . ," says James. Sometimes when problems come we become desperate and use frantic means to cut short the trial. Without consulting the Lord as to His purposes in the matter, we rush to the doctor, for instance, and gulp down large doses of medicine in order to shorten the trial. By doing this, we may actually be thwarting God's program in our lives. And it is just possible that we may have to undergo a longer trial in the future before His particular purpose is realized in us. We should not short-circuit the development of endurance in our lives. By cooperating with God we will become mature, well-rounded Christians, lacking in none of the graces of the Spirit (verse 4).

We should never become despondent or discouraged either when passing through trials. No problem is too great for our Father. Some problems in life are never removed. We must learn

5

to accept them and to prove His grace sufficient. Paul asked the Lord three times to remove a physical infirmity. The Lord did not remove it, but gave Paul grace to bear it (2 Corinthians 12:8-10).

> When through fiery trials thy pathway shall lie,
> My grace, all sufficient, shall be thy supply;
> The flame shall not hurt thee; I only design
> Thy dross to consume, and thy gold to refine.

When we face problems in life that God obviously isn't going to remove, we should be submissive to His will. Fanny Crosby, the blind hymn-writer, wrote these lines as a girl of eight:

> O what a happy soul am I
> Although I cannot see;
> I am resolved that in this world
> Contented I will be.
> How many blessings I enjoy
> That other people don't.
> To weep and sigh because I'm blind
> I cannot and I won't.

Peace comes through submission to the will of God. Some problems in life are removed when we have learned our lessons from them. As soon as the Refiner sees His reflection in the molten metal, He turns off the heat. Most of us lack wisdom to view the pressures of life from God's standpoint. We adopt a short-range view, occupying ourselves with the immediate discomfort. We forget that God's unhurried purpose is to enlarge us through pressure (Psalm 4:1).

We don't have to face the problems of life in our own wisdom. If, in the time of trial, we lack spiritual insight, we should go to God and tell Him all about our perplexity and our ignorance (verse 5). All who are thus exercised to find God's purpose in the trials will be liberally rewarded. And they need not worry that God will scold them either; He is pleased when we are teachable

6

and tractable. We all lack wisdom. The Bible does not give *specific* answers to the innumerable problems that arise in life. It does not solve problems in so many words, but God's Word does give us general principles. We must apply these principles to problems as they arise day by day. That is why we need wisdom. "Spiritual wisdom is the practical application in the daily life of the teaching of Jesus Christ."

We must approach God in faith, with no doubts (verse 6). We must believe He loves and cares, and that nothing is impossible with Him. If we doubt His goodness and His power, we will have no steadfastness in the hour of trouble. One minute we might be resting calmly on His promises, but the next we will feel that God has forgotten to be kind. We will be like the surge of the sea, rising to great heights, then falling back into valleys, troubled and tossed. God is not honored by the kind of faith that alternates between optimism and pessimism. He does not give divine insight to such vacillating, unstable men (verses 7, 8).

Note the following in verses 5-8. The source of wisdom is God; it is obtained by prayer; it is available to all men; it is given liberally and without upbraiding, that is, without reproaching; the crucial condition is that we ask in faith, nothing doubting.

At first glance, verses 9-11 seem to introduce a completely new subject, or at least a parenthesis. James, however, seems to be continuing with the subject of holy trials by giving specific illustrations. Whether a man is poor or rich, he can derive lasting spiritual benefits from the calamities and crises of life. For instance, when a brother of low degree finds himself dissatisfied and discouraged, he can always rejoice that he is an heir of God, and a joint heir with Jesus Christ (verse 9). He can find consolation in the truth that all things are his, and he is Christ's and Christ is God's. The brother of low degree probably has no control over his humble circumstances. There is no reason to believe he is lazy or careless. But God has seen fit to place him in a low income bracket and that is where he has been ever since. Perhaps if he had been rich he never would have accepted Christ. Now that he is in Christ, he is blessed with all spiritual blessings in the heavenlies.

7

What should he do? Should he rebel against his station in life? Should he become bitter and jealous? No, he should accept from God the circumstances over which he has no control and rejoice in his spiritual blessings.

Too many Christians go through life rebelling against their sex, their age, their height and even against life itself. Girls with a flair for baseball wish they were boys. Young people wish they were older, and old people want to be younger. Short people envy those who are tall, and tall ones wish they weren't so conspicuous. Some people even say, "I wish I were dead!" This is absurd! The Christian attitude is to accept from God things which we cannot change. They are God's destiny for us, and we should make the most of them for His glory and for the blessing of others. We should say, with the Apostle Paul, "By the grace of God, I am what I am" (1 Corinthians 15:10). As we forget our disabilities and lose ourselves in service for others, we will come to realize that spiritual people love us for what we are, not for our appearance, for instance.

Next James turns to the rich man. But strangely enough he does not say, "Let the rich man rejoice in his riches." Rather he says that the rich can rejoice that he is made low. He agrees with Jeremiah 9:23, 24: "Let not the wise man glory in his wisdom, neither let the mighty man glory in his might, let not the rich man glory in his riches: but let him that glorieth glory in this, that he understandeth and knoweth me, that I am the Lord which exercise lovingkindness, judgment, and righteousness in the earth: for in these things I delight, saith the Lord."

The rich man may actually find real cause for rejoicing should he be stripped of his material possessions (verses 10, 11). Perhaps business reverses would bring him to the Lord. Or if he is already a Christian, then he could take joyfully the spoiling of his goods knowing he has in heaven a better and more enduring substance (Hebrews 10:34). Earthly riches are destined to pass away, like the flower of the grass (Isaiah 40:6, 7). If a man has nothing but material wealth, then all his plans will end at the grave. James dwells on the transiency of grass as an illustration of the fleeting life of a rich man and the limited value of his riches. He "fades away in his goings," that is, in the midst of his pursuits. The point is, of course, that neither sun nor scorching wind can affect *spiritual* values. Any trial that weans us away from the love of passing things and sets our affections on things above is a blessing in disguise. Thus the same grace that exalts the lowly (verse 9) humbles the rich (verse 10). Both are cause for rejoicing.

In concluding his discussion of holy trials, James pronounces a blessing on the man who stands up under afflictions (verse 12). When such a man has been "approved" (better than "when he is tried," as in the AV) he shall receive the crown of life (ASV). The crown here is the victor's wreath, not the king's diadem. It will be awarded at the Judgment Seat of Christ. There is no suggestion, of course, that eternal life is the reward for enduring testings but those who have endured with fortitude will be honored for that kind of life, and will enjoy a deeper appreciation of eternal life in heaven. Everyone's cup will be full in heaven but people will have different sized cups, that is, different capacities for enjoying heaven. This is doubtless what is in view in the expression "crown of life"; it refers to a fuller enjoyment of the glories of heaven.

Now let us make this section on holy trials practical in our own lives. How do we react when various forms of testing come into our lives? Do we complain bitterly against the misfortunes of life, or do we rejoice and thank the Lord for them? Do we advertise our trials or do we bear them quietly? Do we live in the future, waiting for our circumstances to improve, or do we live in the present, seeking to see the hand of God in all that comes to us? Do we indulge in self-pity and seek sympathy or do we submerge self in a life of service for others?

2. Unholy Temptations (1:13-17)

The subject now shifts to unholy temptations (verses 13-17). Just as holy trials are designed to bring out the best in us, so unholy temptations are designed to bring out the evil in us. One thing must be clearly understood. When we are tempted to sin, the temptation does *not* come from God (verse 13). God does test or try men, as far as their faith is concerned, but He never tempts a man to commit any form of evil. He Himself has no dealings with evil, and He does not entice to sin.

Man is always ready to shift responsibility for his sins. If he cannot blame God, he will adopt the approach of modern psychology by saying that sin is a sickness. In this way he hopes to escape judgment. But sin is not a sickness; it is a moral failure for which man must give account. Some even try to blame inanimate things for sin. But material "things" are not sinful in themselves. Sin does not originate there. James tracks the lion to its den when he says, "Every man is tempted, when he is drawn away of his own lust, and enticed" (verse 14). Sin comes from within us, from our old, evil, fallen, unregenerate nature. Jesus said, "Out of the heart proceed evil thoughts, murders, adulteries, fornications, thefts, false witness, blasphemies" (Matthew 15:19).

Actually the word James uses for *lusts* in verse 14 could refer to any form of desire, good or evil. The word itself is morally neutral. But with few exceptions it is used in the New Testament to describe evil desires, and that is certainly the case here. Lust is likened to an evil woman in verse 14 parading her allurements and enticing her victims. Every one of us is tempted. We have vile lusts and impure appetites constantly urging us on to sin. Are we helpless victims then, when we are drawn away by our own lust and enticed? No, we may expel all thoughts of sin from our mind and concentrate on subjects that are pure and holy (Philippians 4:8). Also in the moment of fierce temptation, we may call on the Lord, remembering that "The Name of the Lord is a strong tower: the righteous runneth into it, and is safe" (Proverbs 18:10).

If that is so, why then do we sin? The answer is in verse 15: " . . . when lust hath conceived, it bringeth forth sin." Instead of expelling the vile thought, we may encourage, nourish and enjoy it. This act of acquiescence is likened to the marriage act. Lust conceives and a hideous baby named SIN is born. Which is another way of saying that if we think about a forbidden act long enough, we will eventually do it. The whole process of lust conceiving and bringing forth sin is vividly illustrated in the incident of David and Bathsheba (2 Samuel 11:1-27).

"And sin, when it is finished, bringeth forth death," says James. Sin is not a barren, sterile thing; it produces a brood of its own. The statement that sin brings forth death may be understood in several ways: First of all, the sin of Adam brought physical death on himself and on all his posterity (Genesis 2:17). But sin also leads to eternal, spiritual death—the final separation of the person from God and from blessing (Romans 6:23a). There is a sense also in which sin results in death for a believer. For instance, in 1 Timothy 5:6 we read that a believing widow who lives in pleasure is dead while she lives. This means that she is wasting her life and utterly failing to fulfill the purpose for which God saved her. To be out of fellowship with God is for a Christian a form of living death.

It is not unusual for men who fall into sin to blame God instead of themselves. They say, in effect, to their Creator, "Why have you made me thus?" But this is a form of self-deception (verse 16). Only good gifts come from God (verse 17). In fact, He is the source of every good and every perfect gift.

James describes God as the Father of lights (v. 17). The word *Father* in the Bible sometimes has the meaning of Creator (see Job 38:28). Therefore God is the Creator or Source of lights. But what is meant by lights? Certainly it includes the heavenly bodies —the sun, moon and stars (Genesis 1:14-18; Psalm 136:7). But God is also the Source of all spiritual light as well. So we should think of Him as the Source of every form of light in the universe "with whom is no variableness, neither shadow of turning." God is unlike the heavenly bodies He has created. They are undergoing constant changes. He never does. Perhaps James is thinking not only of the declining brilliance of the sun and stars, but also of their changing relation to the earth as our planet rotates. Variableness characterizes the sun, the moon and the stars. The expression "neither shadow of turning" may also be translated "neither shadow caused by turning." This could have reference to the shadows cast on earth by the rotation of the earth around the sun.

Or it could refer to eclipses. A solar eclipse, for instance, is produced where the moon's shadow falls on the earth. With God it is quite different; there is no variableness in Him, neither shadow caused by turning. And His gifts are as perfect as Himself. Therefore it is unthinkable that He would ever entice man to sin. Temptation comes from man's own evil nature.

Now let us test our faith on the subject of unholy temptations. Do we encourage evil thoughts to linger in our minds, or do we expel them quickly? When we sin, do we say that we couldn't help it? Do we blame God when we are tempted to sin?

When you have mastered this lesson, take the first part of Exam 1 (covering lesson 1), questions 1-10 on pages 19-21 (right after lesson 2).

Lesson 2

The Living Word (James 1:18-27)

James has been speaking of God as the Father of lights. Now he reminds us that He is our Father also, and that He has given us a unique role in His vast creation. We can fulfill that role by obedience to the Word of Truth (verses 19-27).

THE BIBLE AND SPIRITUAL LIFE (1:18)

This passage really outlines the part played in the new birth by the Word of God as it is applied to us by the Holy Spirit. We are told of God that "of his own free will begat He us by the word of truth, that we should be a kind of firstfruits of His creatures." *Of His own will—* This tells us what prompted Him to save us. He was not forced to do it by any merit in us. He did it of His own free will. His love to us was unmerited, unbought and unsought. It was entirely voluntary on His part. This should cause us to worship! *Begat He us—*This describes the fact of the new birth. He brought us forth or begat us. By this spiritual birth we become His children—a relationship that can never be changed since a birth can never be undone. *By the word of truth—*The Bible is the instrument of the new birth. In every genuine case of conversion, the Scriptures are involved, whether orally or in printed form. Apart from the Bible, we would not know the way of salvation. Indeed, we would not even know that salvation was available! *That we should be a kind of firstfruits of his creatures—*There are three prominent thoughts

13

in connection with the word *firstfruits*. First, the firstfruits of a harvest was the first sheaf of ripened grain. The Christians to whom James was writing were among the first believers in the Christian dispensation. They were a sort of firstfruits. Of course, all believers are a kind of firstfruits of His creatures, but the primary reference is to the Jewish Christians to whom James wrote. Second, the firstfruits were offered to God in gratitude for His bounty and in recognition that all comes from Him and belongs to Him. Thus, all believers should present themselves to God as living sacrifices (Romans 12:1, 2). Third, the firstfruits were a pledge of the full harvest to come. James likened his reader to the first sheaves of grain in the harvest of Christ. They would be followed by others down through the centuries, but they were set forth as pattern saints to exhibit the fruits of the new creation. Eventually the Lord will populate the whole earth with others like them (Romans 8:19-23). The full harvest will come when the Lord Jesus returns to reign over the earth. In the meantime, they were to yield the same kind of obedience to Christ which all the world will yield during the millennium. And though the passage refers primarily to first-century Christians, yet it has an application for each one of us who honors the name of Christ.

OUR RESPONSIBILITY TO THE WORD (1:19-27)

The remaining verses of the chapter give practical instructions as to how we can be firstfruits of His creatures. They set forth the practical righteousness which should characterize those who have been born again by the Word of Truth. We know that we were begotten by the Word in order to manifest the truth of God; now let us discharge our responsibility.

We should be swift to hear (verse 19). This is an unusual command, with almost a trace of humor in it. It's like saying "Hurry up and hear!" It means, of course, that we should be ready to hear the Word of God, as well as all godly counsel and admonition. We should be teachable by the Holy Spirit. We should be slow to speak. It is surprising how much James has to say about our speech. He cautions us to be guarded in our conversation. Even nature itself teaches us this. "Nature has given to man one tongue, but two ears, that we may hear from others twice as much as we speak"—Epictetus. Solomon would have agreed heartily with James. He once said, "He that keepeth his mouth keepeth his life: but he that openeth wide his lips shall have destruction" (Proverbs 13:3). He also said, "In the multitude of words there wanteth not sin: but he that refraineth his lips is wise" (Proverbs 10:19). Compulsive talkers eventually transgress.

We should be slow to wrath. A man who is quick-tempered does not produce the kind of righteousness which God expects from His children (verse 20). Those who lose their temper give people a wrong impression about Christianity. It is still true that "he that is slow to anger is better than the mighty; and he that ruleth his spirit than he that taketh a city" (Proverbs 16:32).

Another way to manifest ourselves as firstfruits of His creatures is by laying aside all filthiness and "superfluity of naughtiness." These vices are likened to soiled garments which are to be set aside once for all. Filthiness includes every form of impurity, whether spiritual, mental or physical. The expression "superfluity of naughtiness" is translated "overflowing of wickedness" in the American Standard Version. It may refer to those forms of evil which are our inheritance from our unconverted days. It may refer to sins which overflow from our lives and touch the lives of others. Or it may refer to abounding evil, in which case James is not so much describing an excess of evil, but the intensely wicked character which evil has. The over-all meaning is clear. In order to receive the truth of the Word of God, we must be morally clean.

Another requirement for the reception of divine truth is meekness. It is all too possible to read the Bible without letting it speak to us. We can study it in an academic way without being affected by it. Our pride and hardness and sin make us unreceptive and unresponsive. Only those with submissive, humble spirits can expect to derive the maximum benefit from the Scriptures. "The meek will he guide in judgment: and the meek will he teach his way" (Psalm 25:9). " . . . to this man will I look, even to him that is poor and of a contrite spirit, and trembleth at my word" (Isaiah 66:2).

James speaks of the Scriptures as "the engrafted word which is able to save your souls." According to this translation, he sees the Word as being joined or fastened to the believer as if by grafting at the time of conversion. Most modern versions prefer the picture of "the implanted Word." Here the thought is that the Word becomes a sacred deposit in the Christian's life when he is born again. The margin of the Revised Version reads "the inborn Word." This Word is able to "save your souls." The Bible is the instrument God uses in the new birth. He uses it in saving the soul not only from the penalty of sin, but from its power as well. He uses it in saving us not only from damnation in eternity, but from damage in this life. It is doubtless this present, continuing aspect of salvation which James is speaking of in verse 21.

It is not enough to receive the implanted Word; we must obey it (verse 22). There is no virtue in possessing the Bible or even in reading it as literature. There must be a deep desire to hear God speaking to us and an unquestioning willingness to do whatever He says. We must translate the Bible into action. The Word must become flesh in our lives. There should never be a time when we go to the Scriptures without allowing them to change our lives for the better. To profess great love for God's Word or even to pose as a Bible student is a form of self-deception unless our increasing knowledge of the Word is producing increasing likeness to the Lord Jesus. To go on gaining an intellectual knowledge of the Bible without obeying it can be a snare instead of a blessing. If we continually learn what we ought to do, but do not do it, we become depressed and frustrated and callous. "Impression without expression leads to depression." Also we become more responsible before God. The ideal combination is to read the Word and obey it implicitly. The man who hears the Word but does not change his behavior is like a man who takes a fleeting glance in the mirror each morning, then completely forgets what he saw (verses 23, 24). He derives no benefit from the mirror or from looking into it. Of course, there are some things about our appearance that cannot be changed. But at least we should be humbled by the sight. And when the mirror says "Wash" or "Shave" or "Comb" or "Brush," we should at least do as we are told. Otherwise the mirror is of no practical benefit to us.

It is so easy to read the Bible casually or because of a sense of duty without being affected by what we read. We see what we ought to be but we quickly forget and live as if we were already perfect. This type of self-satisfaction prevents spiritual progress. In contrast is the man who looks into the Word of God and who habitually reduces it to practice (v. 25). His contemplative, meditative gazing has practical results in his life. To him the Bible is the perfect law of liberty. Its precepts are not burdensome. They tell him to do exactly what his new nature loves to do. As he obeys, he finds true freedom from human traditions and carnal reasonings. The truth makes him free. This is the man who benefits from the Bible. He does not forget what he has read. Rather he seeks to live it out in daily practice. His simple, childlike obedience brings incalculable blessing to his soul. "He shall be blessed in his doing" (RV).

In verses 26 and 27, vain religion and pure religion are contrasted. Religion here means the external patterns of behavior connected with religious belief. It refers to the outward forms rather than the inward spirit. It means the outer expression of belief in worship and service rather than to the doctrines believed.

A man might think himself to be religious, but if he cannot control his tongue, his religion is empty and useless. He might observe all kinds of religious ceremonies which make him appear very pious. But he is deceiving himself. God is not satisfied with rituals; He is interested in a life of practical godliness.

An unbridled tongue is not the only kind of vain religion. It is only one example. Any behavior that is inconsistent with the Christian faith is worthless. The story is told of a pious grocer who apparently was a pious fraud. He lived in an apartment above his store. Every morning he would call down to his assistant, "James!"

"Yes, sir."

"Have you watered the milk?"

"Yes, sir."

"Have you colored the butter?"

"Yes, sir."

"Have you put chicory in the coffee?"

"Yes, sir."

"Very well: come up for morning devotions."

James says that such religion is vain.

What God is looking for is the practical type of godliness which takes a compassionate interest in others and which keeps one's own life clean. As examples of religion that is pure and undefiled, James praises the man who visits needy widows and orphans, and who keeps himself unspotted from the world.

In other words, the practical outworking of the new birth is found in "acts of grace and a walk of separation." Guy King describes these virtues as practical love and practical holiness.

And so at the end of this section we should put our faith on trial with the following questions. Do I read the Bible with a humble desire to have God rebuke me, teach me and change me? Am I anxious to have my tongue bridled? Do I justify my temper or do I want victory over it? How do I react when someone starts to tell an off-color joke? Does my faith manifest itself in deeds of kindness to those who cannot repay me?

When you are ready, complete Exam 1 by answering questions 11-20 on pages 21-23. (You should have already answered questions 1-10 as part of your study of lesson 1.)

Name _____
(print plainly)

Exam
Grade_____

Address _____

City_____ State _____ Zip Code _____ Class Number _____

Instructor _____

LESSON 1

In the blank space in the right-hand margin write the letter of the correct answer.

1. James draws heavily on the Sermon on the Mount in writing his epistle. Which of the following is **NOT** an example of this? His reference to
   a. the single eye
   b. the Bible as a mirror
   c. the royal law
   d. the peacemaker

   C

2. James' style is similar to that found in
   a. the book of Proverbs
   b. Genesis
   c. Paul's epistles
   d. the book of Acts

   D

3. James describes himself as
   a. "the Lord's brother"
   b. "the son of Zebedee"
   c. "the servant of God and of the Lord Jesus Christ"
   d. "the bondslave of Jesus"

   C

4. The epistle of James is addressed to the "twelve tribes scattered abroad." This
   a. refers to the tribes carried into captivity by the Assyrians
   b. refers to the tribes carried into captivity by the Babylonians
   c. refers to the Christians scattered abroad by the persecutions of Saul
   d. could refer to Jews who had been scattered on any of the above occasions

   B

5. James tells us that when we fall into seemingly adverse circumstances we should
   a. weep and mourn
   b. complain to God
   c. rejoice
   d. demand our civil rights

   C

6. Fanny Crosby, who wrote the lines beginning "Oh what a happy soul am I,"
   a. had just received a large legacy
   b. was blind
   c. was a mature saint in her eighties when she wrote
   d. was being sarcastic

   B

7. If we find ourselves perplexed by our circumstances and unable to understand why certain problems and pressures have arisen in our lives we should
   a. consult a psychologist
   b. take a course in business management
   c. ask God for wisdom
   d. adopt a philosophical view of life

   C

8. Which of the following does James say has ground for rejoicing? The
   a. brother who finds himself in humble circumstances
   b. rich man who has just concluded a successful and profitable business deal
   c. the poor believer who has just received a large legacy of money
   d. the young man who has not a worry in the world

   A

9. Temptation to sin
   a. is experienced only by the unsaved
   b. arises from within our own hearts
   c. is a common lot of all of us so we are not really to blame if we yield to it
   d. only rarely comes from God

   B

10. To which of the following does James liken the lust-sin-death process? To
   a. the act of fishing with a lure
   b. the act of sleeping
   c. the act of bribing a judge
   d. the marriage act

WHAT DO YOU SAY?

Describe your circumstances and the way you can see God's hand in them.

_____

_____

_____

_____

_____

LESSON 2

In the blank space in the right-hand margin write the letter of the correct answer.

11. Which of the following is the effective instrument for bringing about the new birth?
   a. Baptism
   b. Church membership
   c. Confirmation
   d. The Word of God

12. James told his generation of Christians that they should be a kind of
   a. sacrament of holiness
   b. firstfruits of God's creation
   c. living epistle
   d. walking Biblical encyclopedia

13. We should be *swift* to
    a. speak for God
    b. pray in public
    c. hear God's Word
    d. stand up for our rights

    C

14. Proverbs 10:19 and Proverbs 13:3 both have which of the following in common with James 1:19? All passages deal with
    a. sins of the tongue
    b. giving to the poor
    c. spending time with God in a daily period of prayer
    d. memorizing Scripture

    A

15. Which of the following is *NOT* absolutely necessary if we are to receive the Word? We must have
    a. moral purity
    b. readiness to hear from God
    c. meekness
    d. a good education

    D

16. Speaking of the "engrafted" or "implanted" word being able to "save our souls" James is most likely referring to the Word of God as it
    a. convicts the sinner of his lost condition
    b. converts the repentant sinner into a child of God
    c. causes the child of God to enter into victory over the power of sin
    d. confounds the reasoning of this world

    A

17. James says that those who are "hearers of the Word" must also be
    a. defenders of the Word
    b. doers of the Word
    c. distributors of the Word
    d. debaters of the Word

    B

18. To which of the following does James liken the man who reads the Bible but ignores its message? To a man who
    a. goes fishing but fails to catch anything
    b. refuses to cook the meat he has taken in hunting
    c. looks into a mirror and then forgets what he saw
    d. buys a book but doesn't read it

19. By "religion" James means

    a. any system of belief which men follow sincerely

    b. only those systems of belief which are based upon the Bible

    c. the external patterns of behavior connected with religious belief

    d. the inward spirit of true worship   *D*

20. Which of the following does James give as an example of "pure religion"?

    a. Reading one's Bible daily

    b. Attending church services regularly

    c. Participating in the ordinances of the church

    d. Taking care of widows and orphans   *D*

WHAT DO YOU SAY?

What is your motive in studying this course?

_____

_____

_____

_____

_____

Lesson 3

Don't Practice Partiality (James 2:1-13)

The first thirteen verses of Chapter 2 denounce the practice of showing respect of persons. Favoritism is utterly foreign to the example of the Lord or to the teachings of the New Testament. There is no place in Christianity for snobbishness or discrimination.

THE PRACTICE FORBIDDEN (2:1)

First of all, the practice is distinctly forbidden (verse 1). Note first that the admonition is addressed to believers; we are assured of this by the salutation, "my brethren." The words "have not" might be paraphrased "hold not" or "practice not." "The faith of the Lord Jesus Christ" refers to the Christian faith. It is not a question of His trust or dependence, but rather of the body of truth which He gave to us. The phrase, "with respect of persons," refers to the unchristian practice of showing partiality. Putting all these thoughts together, we find that James is saying, "My brethren, in your practice of the Christian faith, do not show respect of persons." Snobbery and caste distinctions are utterly inconsistent with true Christianity. Servility to human greatness has no place in the presence of the Lord of Glory. Contempt for others because of birth, race, sex or poverty is a practical denial of the faith. This commandment of course does not contradict other portions of the New Testament where believers are taught to pay proper respect to rulers, masters, elders and parents. There are certain divinely ordained relationships which must be recognized (Romans 13:7). In this passage it is a matter of showing obsequious deference to people because of their expensive clothing or other artificial distinctions.

THE PRACTICE ILLUSTRATED (2:2-4)

This is confirmed by the vivid illustration which James gives in verses 2-4. Guy King has cleverly entitled this section "The Shortsighted Usher." The scene is the local assembly of Christians. (The Revised Version has "synagogue" rather than "assembly." But the primary meaning of "synagogue" is a bringing together, whether of persons or things. Here it means a gathering of people. It does not necessarily mean the building in which the gathering is held.) A distinguished looking gentleman, with fashionable clothing and expensive gold rings has just arrived. The usher bows and scrapes, then escorts the notable visitor to a prominent, conspicuous seat in the front. As soon as the usher gets back to the door, he finds that another visitor has arrived. This time it is a poor man in humble attire. (The expression "vile raiment" does not mean the man is dressed shabbily, or that his clothes needed cleaning. He is dressed simply, in keeping with his humble circumstances in life.) This time the usher adroitly seeks to save the congregation from embarrassment by offering the visitor standing room at the rear, or a place on the floor, in front of his own seat. It seems incredible that anyone would ever act in this way. We would like to think that the illustration is overdrawn, but when we look into our own heart, we find that we often do make these artificial, class distinctions among ourselves, and thus become judges with evil thoughts.

Probably the most glaring example of it in the church today is the discrimination that is shown against people of other races and colors. Negro believers have been ostracized in many instances or at least made to feel unwelcome. Converted Jews have not always been accepted cordially. Oriental Christians have tasted discrimination in varying degrees. It is admitted that there are enormous social problems in the whole area of race relations. But the Christian must be true to divine principles. His obligation is to give practical expression to the truth that all believers are one in Christ Jesus.

THE EVILS OF THE PRACTICE EXPOSED (2:5-11)

Partiality is utterly incongruous with the Christian faith. James demonstrates this in verses 5-13. He gives four strong reasons why it is ridiculous for a believer to favor the rich and look down on the poor.

First of all, it means that we dishonor a man whom God honors (verses 5, 6a). God has chosen the poor people of this world rich in faith, and heirs of the kingdom which He has promised to them that love Him. "The poor are God's elect, God's elite, heirs of God and lovers of God." Repeatedly we find in Scripture that it is the poor people, not the rich, who rally to the banner of Christ. Our Lord Himself said, "The poor have the gospel preached to them" (Matthew 11:5). It was the common people who heard Him gladly, not the wealthy or aristocratic (Mark 12:37). Not many noble are called, but the foolish, the weak, the base, the despised and the insignificant (1 Corinthians 1:26-29). Rich people are ordinarily poor in faith, because they trust their riches instead of the Lord. On the other hand, poor people have been chosen by God to be rich in faith. A survey of the citizens of His kingdom would reveal that most of them have been poor. In the kingdom, they will occupy positions of wealth and glory. How foolish, then, and how perilous it is to treat with contempt those who will one day be exalted in the kingdom of our Lord and Savior.

A second reason why it is foolish to show deference to the rich is that, as a class, they are the ones who have characteristically oppressed the people of God (verse 6b). The argument is involved, and even a little confusing at this point. The rich man referred to earlier in the chapter was undoubtedly a believer. That does not mean that the rich men mentioned in verse 6 are believers also. What James is saying is simply this: "Why show favoritism to people just because they are rich? If you do, you are honoring those who have been the first to bully you and to drag you into court." Calvin captured the argument tersely when he said, "Why honor your executioners?"

A third reason why it is foolish to be partial toward the rich is that they habitually use evil or harsh speech involving the Name of Christ. This is the worthy Name by which believers are called—Christians, or followers of Christ. While railing against the Lord is not a sin on which the rich have a monopoly, yet it is true that those who persecute poor believers often accompany this persecution with the vilest language against the Savior. So why should believers show special favoritism toward anyone simply because he is wealthy; the traits which accompany riches are not ordinarily honoring to the Lord Jesus. The expression "that worthy Name by which ye are called" might also be translated "that worthy Name which has been called upon you." Some see in this a reference to Christian baptism. Believers are baptized in the Name of the Lord Jesus. This is the very Name which the rich habitually blaspheme.

James' fourth argument is that showing deference to the rich violates the law of love (verse 8). The law of love is "Thou shalt love thy neighbor as thyself." If we really loved our neighbors as ourselves, we would treat them the way we would want to be treated. Certainly *we* would not want to be despised simply because we were poor. Then we should not show contempt to others for this reason.

Of all the teachings of the New Testament, this is certainly one of the most revolutionary—"Thou shalt love thy neighbor as thyself." Think what it means! It means that we should care for others as we care for ourselves. We should be willing to share our material possessions with those who are not as privileged as we are. And above all, we should do all in our power to see that they have the opportunity to know our blessed Savior. Too often our decisions are based on how our actions affect ourselves. We are self-centered. We cater to the rich because of the hope of reward, either socially or materially. We neglect the poor because there is little prospect of their benefiting us in any way. The royal law forbids such selfish exploitation of others. It teaches us to love our neighbor as ourselves. And if we ask, "Who is my neighbor?" we learn from the story of the Good Samaritan (Luke 10:29-37) that our neighbor is any person who has a need which we can help to meet.

The law of love is called the royal law (verse 8) because it belongs to the King and because it is the king of all laws. To show respect of persons is a violation of the royal law (verse 9). It is both sin and transgression. Sin is any lack of conformity to the will of God, a failure to meet His standards. Transgression is the breaking of a known law. Certain acts are sinful because they are basically and inherently wrong, but they become transgressions when there is a specific law which forbids them. Partiality is sinful because it is essentially wrong in itself. But it is also transgression because there is a law against it. To break one part of the law is to be guilty of all (verse 10). The law is like a chain of ten links. Break one link and the chain is broken. God does not allow us to keep the laws we like, and break others. The same God who forbade adultery also forbade murder (verse 11). A man may not be guilty of adultery, yet he may commit murder. Is he a transgressor of the law? Certainly he is! The spirit of the law is that we should love our neighbor as ourselves. Adultery is certainly a violation of this, but so is murder. And so is snobbishness and discrimination. If we commit any of these sins, we have failed to do what the law commands.

Now we must pause in our discussion to consider a basic problem which arises at this point in James' argument. The problem is this, "Are Christians under the law or are they not?" It certainly seems that James has been enforcing the Ten Commandments on Christian believers. He specifically refers to the sixth and seventh commandments which forbid murder and adultery. Also he summarizes the last five commandments in the words, "Thou shalt love thy neighbor as thyself." Yet to put believers under the law, as a rule of life contradicts other portions of the New Testament, such as Romans 6:14, "Ye are not under law, but under grace"; Romans 7:6, "We are delivered from the law"; Romans 7:4, "Ye are become dead to the law by the body of Christ." See also Galatians 2:19; 3:13; 3:24, 25; 1 Timothy 1:8, 9; Hebrews 7:19. The fact that Christians are not under the Ten Commandments is distinctly stated in 2 Corinthians 3:7-11.

Why then does James press the matter of the law on believers in this age of grace? First of all, Christians are *not* under the law as a rule of life. Christ, not the law, is the believer's pattern. Where there is law, there must also be penalty. The penalty for breaking the law is death.

Christ died to pay the penalty, of the broken law. Those who are in Christ are therefore delivered from the law and its penalty. But certain principles of the law *are* of abiding value. These precepts apply to all people of all ages. Idolatry, adultery, murder and theft are basically and inherently wrong. They are just as wrong for believers as for unbelievers. Moreover, nine of the Ten Commandments are repeated in the Epistles. The only one that is not repeated is the one concerning the Sabbath. Nowhere are Christians ever told to keep the Sabbath or seventh day of the week for that commandment is ceremonial rather than moral. It was not basically wrong in itself for a Jew to work on the seventh day. It was wrong only because God set that day apart.

Finally it should be mentioned that the nine commandments which are repeated in the Epistles are not given as *law* but as instruction in righteousness for the people of God. In other words, God does not say to Christians, "If you steal, you are condemned to death." Or "If you commit an immoral act, you will lose your salvation." Rather He says, "I have saved you by my grace. Now I want you to live a holy life out of love to me. If you want to know what I expect of you, you will find it throughout the New Testament. There you will find nine of the Ten Commandments repeated. But you will also find the teachings of the Lord Jesus which actually call for a higher standard of conduct than the law required." James is not really putting believers under the law and its condemnation. He is not saying, "If you show respect of persons, you are breaking the law, and are thus condemned to death." What he is saying is, "As believers, you are no longer under the law of bondage, but you are under the law of liberty—liberty to do what is right. The law of Moses required you to love your neighbor but did not give you the power, and condemned you if you failed. Under grace, you are given the power to love your neighbor and are rewarded when you do it. You don't do it in order to be saved but because you are saved. You do it, not through fear of punishment, but through love for Him who died for you and rose again. When you stand before the Judgment Seat of Christ, you will be rewarded or suffer loss according to this standard. It will not be a question of salvation but of reward."

DON'T BE PARTIAL (2:12-13)

The expression "So speak ye, and so do" refers to words and deeds (verse 12). Both profession and life should agree. In speech and act, believers should avoid partiality. Such violations of the law of liberty will be judged at the Judgment Seat of Christ.

Verse 13 must be understood in the light of the context. James is speaking to believers. There is no question of eternal punishment of sins here; that penalty was paid once for all at Calvary's cross. Here it is a question of God's dealing with us in this world as His children. If we do not show mercy to others, we are not walking in fellowship with God and can expect to suffer the consequences of a backslidden condition.

The expression "and mercy rejoiceth against judgment" may mean that God would rather show mercy to us than discipline us (Micah 7:18); judgment is His "strange work." It may mean we can rejoice in the face of judgment if we have shown mercy to others, but if we have not shown mercy to those whom we might justly condemn, we will not be shown mercy. Or it may mean that mercy triumphs over judgment in the sense that it is always greater than judgment. The general idea seems to be that if we show mercy to others, the judgment which might otherwise fall on us will be replaced by mercy.

Let us test ourselves then on this important subject of partiality. Do we show more kindness to those of our own race than those of other races? Are we more kindly disposed to the young than to the old? Are we more outgoing to good-looking people than to those who are plain or homely? Are we more anxious to befriend prominent people than those who are comparatively unknown? Do we avoid people with physical infirmities and seek the companionship of the strong and healthy? Do we favor the rich over the poor? Do we give the "cold shoulder" to "foreigners," those who speak our language with a foreign accent?

As we answer these questions, let us remember that the way we treat the least lovable believer is the way we treat the Savior (Matthew 25:40).

When you have mastered this lesson, take the first part of Exam 2 (covering lesson 3), questions 1-10 on pages 41-42 (right after lesson 2).

Lesson 4

Faith and Works (James 2:14-26)

These verses are perhaps the most controversial in the epistle by James. Even such a great worthy of the church as Luther thought he saw an irreconcilable conflict between James' teaching on justification by works and Paul's insistence on justification by faith. These verses are commonly used to support the heresy that we are saved by faith plus works. In other words, we must trust the Lord Jesus as our Savior, but that is not enough. We must also add to His redemptive work our own deeds of charity and devotion. The section might actually be titled "Justification by Works," because there is a sense in which we *are* justified by works. In fact, in order to grasp the full truth of justification, we should clearly understand that we are justified by *grace* (Romans 3:24). This simply means that we do not deserve to be justified; in fact, we deserve the very opposite. We are justified by *faith* (Romans 5:1). Faith is the human response to God's grace. By faith, we accept the free gift. Faith is that which appropriates what God has done for us. We are justified by *blood* (Romans 5:9). Here blood is the price which had to be paid in order to procure our justification. The debt of sin was met by the precious blood of Christ, and now God can justify ungodly sinners because a righteous satisfaction has been made. We are justified by *God* (Romans 8:33). The truth here is that God is the Person who justifies. And we are justified by *works* (James 2:24). Works are the outward proof of the reality of our faith. They give outward expression to what would otherwise be invisible. From this we see that the person is justified by grace, by faith, by blood, by God and by works. Yet there is no contradiction at all. These statements simply present different aspects of the same truth. Grace is the principle upon which God justifies; faith is the means by which man receives it; blood is the price which the Savior had to pay; God is the active Agent in justification; and works are the result.

This is beautifully expressed in the following lines by Helen Shaw:

> God's sov'reign grace selected me
> To have in heav'n a place;
> 'Twas the good pleasure of His will;
> I'm justified by grace.
>
> In due time Christ on Calv'ry died;
> There flowed that crimson flood
> Which makes the foulest white as snow;
> I'm justified by blood.
>
> God raised Him up; this is the pledge,
> Should evil doubtings low'r,
> His resurrection quells each fear;
> I'm justified by pow'r.
>
> The Holy Spirit guided me
> To what the Scripture saith;
> I grasped the truth; Christ died for me!
> I'm justified by faith.
>
> Now if you doubt that I am Christ's,
> If one suspicion lurks,
> I'll show by deed that I am His,
> I'm justified by works.
>
> I praise the Lord, 'tis all of Him,
> The grace, the faith, the blood,
> The resurrection pow'r, the works,
> I'm justified by God.

FAITH WITHOUT WORKS IS POWERLESS (2:14)

James insists that a faith that does not result in good works cannot save. There are two keys which greatly help in the understanding of this verse. First of all, James does not say "What doth it profit . . . though a man *hath* faith. . . ." Rather, he says, "What doth it profit . . . though a man *say* he hath faith. . . ." In other words, it is not a question of a man who truly *has* faith, and yet is not saved. James is describing the man who has nothing but a profession of faith. He *says* he has faith, but there is nothing about his life that indicates it. The second helpful key is brought out in the American Standard Version. There, the verse closes with the question "Can *that* faith save him?" In other words, can *that kind of faith* save? If it be asked what kind of faith James is referring to, the answer is found in the first part of the verse. He is speaking about a *say-so faith* that is not backed up by good works. Such a faith is worthless. It is all words, and nothing else.

FAITH WITHOUT WORKS ILLUSTRATED (2:15-16)

The futility of words without deeds is now illustrated. We are introduced to two people. One has neither adequate food nor clothing. The other has both, but is not willing to share them. Professing great generosity, he says to his poor brother, "Go and put on some clothing, and eat a good meal." But he doesn't raise a little finger to make this possible. What good are such words? They are positively worthless! They neither satisfy the appetite nor provide warmth for the body.

FAITH WITHOUT WORKS IS DEAD (2:17)

Thus faith, if it has not works, is dead in itself (verse 17, ASV). A faith without works is not real faith at all. It is only a matter of words. James is not saying that we are saved by faith *plus* works. To hold such a view would be to dishonor the finished work of the Lord Jesus Christ. If we were saved by faith and by works, then there would be two saviors—

Jesus and ourselves. But the New Testament is very clear that Christ is the one and only Savior. What James is emphasizing is that we are not saved by a faith of works only but by that kind of faith which results in a life of good works. In other words, works are not the root of salvation but the fruit; they are not the cause but the effect.

FAITH AND WORKS ARE INSEPARABLE (2:18)

True faith and good works are inseparable. James shows this by giving us a snatch from a debate between two men. The first man, who is genuinely saved, is the speaker. The second professes to have faith, but he does not demonstrate that faith by good works. The first is heard delivering an unanswerable challenge to the other. We might paraphrase the conversation: "Yes," the first man may correctly and justifiably say, "you say you have faith, but you do not have works to demonstrate it. I claim that faith must be backed up by a life of good works. Prove to me that you have faith without a life of good works. You cannot do it. Faith is invisible. The only way others can know you have faith is by a life that demonstrates it. I will show you my faith by my works." The key to this verse lies in the word *show*: "*Show* me thy faith without thy works, and I will *show* thee my faith by my works." To show faith apart from works is an impossibility.

MENTAL ASSENT IS NOT ENOUGH (2:19-20)

The debate continues. The first man is still the speaker. A man's professed faith may be nothing more than mental assent to a well known fact. Such intellectual agreement involves no committal of the person, and does not produce a transformed life. It is not enough to believe in the existence of God. True, this is essential, but it is not sufficient. Even the demons believe in the existence of God and they shudder at the thought of their eventual punishment by Him. The demons believe the fact, but they do not surrender to the Person. This is not saving faith. When a person truly believes on the Lord, it involves a complete commitment—spirit, soul and body. Then this commitment in turn results in a changed life. Faith apart from works is head belief, and is barren.

TWO EXAMPLES (2:21-25)

Two examples of the faith that works are now given from the Old Testament. They involve Abraham, a Jew, and Rahab, a Gentile. Abraham was justified by works in offering up Isaac his son upon the altar. In order to see this truth in its proper perspective, turn to Genesis 15:6. We read that Abraham believed in the Lord, and He counted it to him for righteousness. Here Abraham was justified by believing; in other words, he was justified by faith. It is not till we come to Genesis 22 that we find Abraham offering up his son. It is then that he was justified by works. As soon as Abraham believed in the Lord, he was justified in the sight of God. But then, seven chapters later, God put Abraham's faith to the test. Abraham demonstrated that it was genuine faith by his willingness to offer up Isaac. His obedience showed that his faith was not merely a head belief, but a heart commitment.

It has sometimes been objected that there was no one else present when Abraham offered up Isaac, and there was therefore no one to whom he could prove the reality of his faith. But the young men who had accompanied Abraham were not far away, waiting for Abraham and Isaac to return from the mount. Moreover, Isaac was there. Also, Abraham's willingness to slay his son in obedience to the Word of God has been preserved in the Bible record, thus demonstrating to all generations the reality of his faith.

It is clear then that Abraham's faith inspired his works, and by his works his faith was made perfect. True faith and works are inseparable. The first produces the second, and the second evidences the first. In the offering of Isaac we see a practical demonstration of the faith of Abraham. It was the practical fulfillment of the Scripture which said that Abraham was justified by believing. His good works identified him as a friend of God.

We conclude from this, then, that a man is justified by works, and not only by faith (verse 24). Again, this does *not* mean that he was justified by faith plus works. He was justified by faith Godward, and by works manward. God justified him the moment he believed. Man says, "Show me the reality of your faith." The only way this can be done is by good works.

The second illustration from the Old Testament is Rahab, the harlot (verse 25). She certainly was not saved by good character because she was a harlot. But she was justified by works because she received the messengers (or spies) and sent them out another way. Rahab was a Canaanite, living in the city of Jericho. She heard reports that a victorious army was advancing toward the city, and that no opposition had been successful against this army. She concluded that the God of the Hebrews was the true God, and decided to identify herself with this God, whatever the cost might be. When the spies entered the city, she befriended them. In doing so, she proved the genuineness of her faith in the true and living God. She was not saved by harboring the spies, but this act of hospitality proved that she was a genuine believer.

Some people use this passage to prove that salvation is by good works. But what they mean by good works is giving to charity, paying your debts, telling the truth and going to church. Were these the good works of Abraham and Rahab? They certainly were not. In Abraham's case, it was willingness to kill his son! In Rahab's case, it was treason! If you remove faith from these works, they would be evil rather than good. "Strip them of faith and they were not only immoral and unfeeling, but they would have been sinful." Mackintosh well says, "This section refers to life-works, not law-works. If you abstract faith from Abraham's and Rahab's works, they were bad works. Look at them as the fruit of faith and they were life-works."

This, then, is not a passage that can be used to teach salvation by good works. It puts the user in the untenable position of teaching salvation by murder and treason.

FAITH IS INANIMATE WITHOUT WORKS (2:26)

The passage ends with the statement, "For as the body without the spirit is dead, so faith without works is dead also" (verse 26). Here the matter is summarized very beautifully. James compares faith to the human body. He likens works to the spirit. The body without the spirit is lifeless, useless, valueless. So faith without works is dead, ineffective, worthless. Obviously it is a spurious faith, not genuine saving faith.

To summarize, then, James tests our faith by our answers to the following questions. Do I keep a modest wardrobe in order to share clothing with those who do not have enough? Do I economize on food in order to help those who are hungry? Do I live sacrificially in order to be able to send the gospel to those who are starving for the Bread of Life? Am I willing like Abraham to offer the dearest thing in my life to God? Am I willing like Rahab to turn traitor to the world in order to be loyal to Christ?

When you are ready, complete Exam 2 by answering questions 11-20 on pages 43-44. (You should have already answered questions 1-10 as part of your study of lesson 3.)

Name_____

(print plainly)

Exam
Grade_____

Address _____

City_____ State _____ Zip Code _____ Class Number _____

Instructor _____

LESSON 3

In the blank space in the right-hand margin write the letter of the correct answer.

1. The warning against partiality is addressed to
a. rich people
b. poor people
c. unbelievers
d. Christians

_D_

2. When James refers to "the faith of the Lord Jesus Christ," he is referring to
a. the faith the Lord Jesus exercised when He lived on earth
b. the faith the Lord Jesus now has in His own
c. the faith which true believers have in the Lord
d. the body of truth given to us by the Lord

_A_

3. Refusing to show partiality means we should
a. act as a slave to rulers only
b. treat all who are in authority with disrespect
c. give those in authority their rightful respect but without being their slave
d. practice discrimination only in racial matters

_C_

4. During His earthly ministry the Lord Jesus was most readily accepted by
a. the common people
b. the ruling classes
c. the wealthy
d. the upper middle class
e. the white Anglo-Saxon protestants

_A_

5. James says that the Lord's people have habitually been oppressed by
   a. rich people
   b. ignorant people
   c. poor people
   d. sincere people

   A

6. James says that showing deference to the rich violates
   a. the Ten Commandments
   b. the law of love
   c. the ecumenical movement
   d. the law of the land

   B

7. If we keep all the commandments of God but break just one of them we
   a. have really done quite well
   b. have merited salvation
   c. have become guilty of all of them
   d. are better than most people

   C

8. The believer in Christ is
   a. not obliged to keep any of the Ten Commandments
   b. not under law but under grace
   c. obliged to keep all the commandments because he is still under law
   d. free from even the spirit of the Old Testament law

   B

9. Which one of the Ten Commandments is *NOT* repeated in the epistles? The commandment concerning
   a. idolatry
   b. covetousness
   c. honoring one's parents
   d. the Sabbath Day

   D

10. The words "he shall have judgment without mercy that hath showed no mercy"
   a. is addressed to unsaved people
   b. proves a Christian can lose his salvation
   c. is a warning to believers that walking out of fellowship with God leads to punishment
   d. is an incorrect translation of the original text

   A

WHAT DO YOU SAY?

Have you ever been the victim of partiality? Describe how you felt.

_____

_____

_____

_____

_____

LESSON 4

In the blank space in the right-hand margin write the letter of the correct answer.

11. Romans 5:1 tells us we are justified by
   a. grace
   b. faith
   c. blood
   d. God

   B

12. The divine side of justification is set forth in the epistle
   a. to the Romans
   b. to the Ephesians
   c. of Peter
   d. of James

   A

13. To say that we are justified by *blood* is to emphasize
   a. the means of justification
   b. the principle of justification
   c. the price of justification
   d. the evidence of justification

   C

14. The key to understanding James 2:14 is in the expression
   a. "what doth it profit"
   b. "my brethren"
   c. "though a man say"
   d. "he hath faith"

   A

15. The American Standard Version sheds light on James 2:14 by adding the word
  a. "therefore"
  b. "that"
  c. "thus"
  d. "thoughtless"

A

16. In the illustration James uses, the wealthy man
  a. congratulated the poor man on his condition which develops spiritual blessing
  b. ignores the poor man altogether
  c. tells the poor man to put on some good clothes and eat well but does nothing to make this possible
  d. gives the poor man the means to be clothed and fed but forgets to tell him what the financial gift is for

C

17. Which of the following is true of the demons? They
  a. really do not exist; all human oddities and abnormalities are psychological
  b. do not believe in the existence of God
  c. do believe in the existence of God but do not surrender to Him although they tremble at their coming doom
  d. do believe in God and will one day be saved because of this

C

18. Abraham was "justified by faith" when he
  a. believed in the Lord
  b. offered up Isaac
  c. married Hagar
  d. cast out the bondwoman and her son

B

19. Rahab was "justified by works" when she
  a. accepted the tidings of Israel's God at face value
  b. befriended the spies
  c. married Salmon
  d. fled from Jericho

B

20. The element which made the works of Abraham and Rahab "life works" instead of "law works" was the element of
  a. faith
  b. hope
  c. love
  d. peace

A

44

WHAT DO YOU SAY?

Give one example of your faith being expressed in works.

_____

_____

_____

_____

_____

Sins of the Tongue (James 3:1-12)

The first twelve verses of Chapter 3 deal with the subject of the tongue. (It is also mentioned in 1:19, 26; 2:12; 4:11; 5:12.) Just as an old fashioned doctor examined a patient's tongue to assist in diagnosis, so James tests a person's spiritual health by his conversation. Self-diagnosis begins with sins of speech. James would agree with the modern wit who said, "Watch your tongue. It is in a wet place where it is easy to slip."

THE TEACHER'S RESPONSIBILITIES (3:1)

The subject is introduced by a warning against the hasty desire to be a teacher of the Word of God. Although the tongue is not specifically mentioned, the underlying thought is that one who uses his tongue in teaching the Scriptures assumes added responsibility before God and man. The words "Be not many masters" may be paraphrased "Do not become unduly ambitious to be a teacher." This should not be interpreted as a prohibition against the use of his gift by one who has actually been called of God to teach. It is a simple warning that this ministry should not be undertaken lightly. Those who teach the Word of Truth will receive heavier judgment if they fail to practice what they teach.

It is a great responsibility to teach the Bible. The teacher must be prepared to obey what he sees in the Word. He can never hope to lead others beyond what he himself has practiced. The extent of his influence on others will be determined by how much he himself has progressed. The teacher begets others in his own image; he makes them like himself. If he dilutes or explains away the clear meaning of any Scripture, he hinders the growth of his students. If he condones sin in any form, he fosters lives of unholiness. No other book makes such claims on its readers as the New Testament. It calls for total commitment to Jesus Christ. It insists that He must be Lord of every phase of the believer's life. It is a serious matter to teach from such a book.

CONTROL OF THE TONGUE IS BASIC (3:2)

James now moves from the specific ministry of teaching to the general area of conversation. We are all prone to stumble in many areas of life but if any man can control his tongue, so that he does not commit the various sins of speech, that man is truly well-rounded and well-disciplined. If a man can exercise control in his speech, he should not have difficulty in practicing self-control in other areas of his life as well. Of course, the Lord Jesus Christ is the only One who ever did this completely, but there is a sense in which each of us can become perfect, that is, mature, complete, thoroughly disciplined.

FIVE ILLUSTRATIONS (3:3-8)

Five figures of speech, or pictures of the tongue are now given. First of all, it is compared to a bridle (verse 3). The bridle is the harness which goes over the head of a horse and which holds the bit in the horse's mouth. Connected to the bit are the reigns. Though the bit itself is a very small piece of steel, yet if a person can control that bit, he can control the behavior of the horse. So the tongue can direct the life—either for good or for evil.

The second picture is that of a rudder (verse 4). Compared with the ship itself, a rudder is small. It weighs only a fraction of the weight of the ship. For example, the Queen Elizabeth weighed 83,673 gross tons. The rudder of that ship weighed only 140 tons—less than two tenths of one percent of the total. Yet when the rudder is turned, it controls the direction of the ship itself. It seems incredible that a man can control so huge a vessel with such a relatively small device; yet this is exactly what happens. Thus we should not misjudge the power of the tongue by its size. Though it is a very small member of the body, and relatively hidden, yet it can boast of great accomplishments, both good and evil.

A third simile of the tongue is a fire (verses 5, 6). A lighted match, carelessly thrown, may start a brush fire. This in turn may ignite a forest and leave a charred mass of ruins. What possibilities, then, a small match holds of destruction and devastation! One of the greatest fire catastrophes of history was the Chicago conflagration of 1871. The tradition persists that it was started when Mrs. O'Leary's cow kicked over her lantern. Whether or not that was true, the fire burned for three days over three and one half square miles of the city. It killed 250 people, made 100,000 homeless, and destroyed property valued at $175,000,000. The tongue is like a small lighted match or a turned-over lantern. Its potentialities for wickedness are almost infinite. James speaks of it as the "world of iniquity" among our members. The word *world* here is used to express vastness. We sometimes use it in this sense; for example, a world full of trouble. We mean a tremendous amount of trouble. The tongue, though so small, has vast possibilities of iniquity in it.

The manner in which the flame of evil speaking spreads is illustrated by the conversation between two women in Brooklyn. One said, "Tilly told me that you told her that secret I told you not to tell her." The other replied, "She's a mean thing. I told Tilly not to tell you I told her." The first speaker responded, "Well, I told Tilly I wouldn't tell you she told me—so don't tell her I did."

The tongue can defile the whole body. We understand this to mean that a person can corrupt his whole personality by using his tongue to slander, abuse, lie, blaspheme and swear.

"The faultfinder injures himself. . . . The mud slinger cannot engage in his favorite pastime without getting some of the mud that he slings both upon his hands and upon his heart. How often we have come away from such an experience with a sense of defilement! Yet that was not our intention at all. We were vainly hoping that by slinging mud upon others we might enhance some one's estimate of our own cleanliness. We were foolish enough to believe that we could build ourselves up by tearing another down. We were blind enough to imagine that by putting a stick of dynamite under the house of our neighbor we could strengthen the foundations of our own. But this is never the case. In our efforts to injure others we may succeed, but we always inflict the deeper injury upon ourselves."[1]

The tongue sets on fire the course of nature, or as the ASV renders it, the wheel of nature (verse 6). This is the wheel set in motion at birth. It describes the whole round of human activity. An evil tongue pollutes not only a man's personal life, but it contaminates all his activities as well. It affects "the whole of wickedness in the whole of man for the whole of life." A wicked tongue is set on fire by hell. All evil speech has its source there. It is hellish in its very character. The word used for hell here is Gehenna; apart from this instance, it was used only by the Lord Jesus in the New Testament.

The fourth figure to which the tongue is likened is a wild, untamable creature (verses 7, 8a). All kinds of beasts, birds, serpents and marine life can be tamed. It is not uncommon to see tame elephants, lions, tigers, birds of prey, serpents, porpoises, and even fish. Pliny lists among creatures that were tamed by men in his day, elephants, lions and tigers, among beasts; the eagle, among birds; asps and other serpents; crocodiles and various fishes, among the inhabitants of the water. To argue that not every kind of creature has actually been tamed is to miss the point of James' argument; there is no reason to believe there is any kind of creature that could not be tamed by man, given sufficient time and persistence.

"What has man done with huge elephants? He has invaded their jungle homes, trapped them, trained them—scores of them—and employed them in carrying lumber, in pushing heavily laden wagons,

---

[1] Clovis G. Chappel, *Sermons from the Psalms* (Nashville: Cokesbury Press, 1931), p. 132.

in all kinds of labor. What has man done with many green-eyed Bengal tigers? He has caught them, taught them, and made them his playmates. What has man done with fierce, furious, strong African lions? He has captured numbers of them and has trained them to jump through hoops of fire, to ride horseback, to sit on high pedestals, to leave untouched—when hungry—beef placed between their paws, to lie down, to stand up, to run, to roar, in obedience to man's spoken word, in obedience to the crack of man's whip. Why, once I, even I, years ago at a circus, saw a lion open wide his cavernous and ravenous mouth and hold it open while a man, his trainer, thrust his head far down into the lion's mouth and held it there a full minute.

"What has man done with the huge boa-constrictor? With the great python? Go to the circus and see little women, frail as flowers, coil these hideous monsters about their bodies with impunity. Go to the animal show, consider how man has made the spotted leopard and the blood-thirsty jaguar harmless and dumb before him. Go to the show and see the trained fleas, see the hungry jackal lie down with the meek lamb, see the dove and the eagle nest together, see the wolf and the rabbit romp in play."[1]

But man's success with wild animals does not extend to the area of his own tongue. If we are honest, we will have to admit that this is true in our own lives. Because of the fall, we have lost dominion over this small piece of flesh. Human nature does not have the ability or strength to govern this little member. Only God can bring it under control.

James next characterizes the tongue as an unruly evil (verse 8). Linking this expression with the words "full of deadly poison" we suspect that James has in mind a restless serpent, with exceedingly poisonous venom. A drop or two would be fatal. So the tongue can poison minds, and assassinate characters. We all know how easy it is to gossip about others. How often we have engaged in mudslinging in order to get even for supposed wrongs. And often for no reason at all we have belittled others, criticized them, downgraded them. Who can measure the harm that has been done, the tears that have flowed, the

---

[1] Robert G. Lee, *Lord I Believe* (Nashville: Broadman Press, 1927), pp. 166-168.

hearts that have been broken, the reputations that have been ruined. And who can measure the misery it has brought to our own lives and to our families? The inward bitterness that has been aroused, the shame of having to apologize, the bad effects on our physical health. Parents who have openly indulged in criticism of fellow-believers have had to watch their children adopt the same critical spirit and wander off from Christian fellowship. The price we have to pay for the undisciplined use of our tongue is enormous.

What is the remedy? Pray daily that the Lord will keep us from gossip, censoriousness and unkind speech. Don't talk unfavorably about anyone; love covers a multitude of sins (1 Peter 4:8). If we have something against another person, let us go to him directly, discuss it in love, and pray together (Matthew 18:15; Luke 17:3). Let us try to see Christ in our brethren instead of magnifying minor failures. If we start to say something unkind or unprofitable, let us stop in the middle of the sentence and explain that to continue wouldn't be edifying.

SPEECH SHOULD ALWAYS BE GOOD (3:9-12)

Next we are taught the inconsistency of using the tongue for both good and evil purposes. It is completely unnatural; there is nothing like it in nature. One minute a man blesses God with his tongue, the next he curses those who are made in the image of God (verse 9). How incongruous it is that a common source should ever produce such opposite results! Such a state of affairs should not exist (verse 10). The tongue that blesses God should help men instead of wounding them. All that we say should be subject to the threefold test: Is it true? Is it kind? Is it necessary? Constantly we should ask the Lord to set a watch before our lips (Psalm 141:3), and pray that the words of our mouths and the meditations of our hearts might be acceptable in the sight of Him who is our strength and our Redeemer (Psalm 19:14). We should remember that our members in Romans 12:1 include our tongue.

No fountain gives pure water and polluted water at the same time (verse 11). The tongue should not do so either. Its outflow should be uniformly good. Just as the water from a fountain speaks of refreshment, so the fruit from a fig tree speaks of nourishment. A fig tree cannot produce olives, neither can a vine yield figs (verse 12a). In nature, a tree produces only one kind of fruit. How is it, then, that the tongue can produce two kinds of fruit—good and evil?

This passage should not be confused with a similar one in Matthew 7:16-20. There we are warned against expecting good fruit from bad trees. Evil men can only produce wicked works. Here we are warned against using the tongue to produce two opposite kinds of fruit. No fountain yields salt water and fresh water at the same time (verse 12b). It must be one or the other. These lessons from nature are intended to remind us that our speech should be consistently good.

Thus, James put us on trial as far as our speech is concerned. Before leaving this section, let us ask ourselves the following questions. Do I teach others things that I have not obeyed myself? Do I criticize others behind their back? Is my speech consistently clean, edifying, kind? Do I use minced oaths such as gosh, golly, gee, jeepers, good heavens, heck? After a solemn meeting, do I engage in levity? Talk about football scores? Do I pun on the Scriptures? In retelling a story, do I exaggerate in order to make people more impressed?

When you have mastered this lesson, take the first part of Exam 3 (covering lesson 5), questions 1-10 on pages 61-62 (right after lesson 6).

Wisdom (James 3:13-18)

James now discusses the difference between true wisdom and false. When James speaks about wisdom, he is not thinking of how much knowledge a man has in his head, but how he lives his life from day to day. It is not the possession of knowledge but the proper application of it that counts. We have here a portrait of the truly wise man. Basically, of course, this man is the Lord Jesus Christ; He is wisdom incarnate (Matthew 11:19; 1 Corinthians 1:30). Then too the truly wise man is the one who manifests the life of Christ, the man in whom the fruit of the Spirit is evident (Galatians 5:22, 23).

We have also a portrait of the worldly-wise man. He acts according to the principles of this world. He embodies all the traits that men glorify. His behavior gives no evidence of divine life within.

THE TRULY WISE MAN (3:13)

If a man is wise and understanding, he will demonstrate it by his good life coupled with the humble spirit that comes from true wisdom (verse 13). The Lord Jesus, the embodiment of true wisdom, was not proud and arrogant; He was meek and lowly in heart (Matthew 11:29). Therefore, all who are truly wise will have the hallmark of genuine humility.

THE WORLDLY-WISE MAN (3:14-16)

The worldly-wise man is characterized by bitter jealousy and selfish ambition in his heart. He has one passion in his life and that is to advance his own interests. He is jealous of any competitors and ruthless in dealing with them. He is proud of his wisdom that has brought success. But James says that this isn't wisdom at all. Such boasting is empty. It is a practical denial of the truth that the man who is truly wise is truly humble (verse 14).

Even in Christian service, it is possible to have a bitter jealousy of other workers, and to seek a prominent place for one's self. There is always a danger that worldly-wise men will be given places of leadership in the church. We must constantly guard against allowing worldly principles to guide us in spiritual affairs. James calls this false wisdom earthly, sensual and devilish (verse 15). There is an intended downward climax in these three adjectives. Earthly means that this wisdom is not from heaven; it is from this earth. Sensual means that it is not the fruit of the Holy Spirit, but of man's lower nature. Devilish means that it stoops to actions that resemble the behavior of demons rather than of men.

Whenever you find jealousy and strife, you will also find disorder, disharmony and every other kind of evil (verse 16). How true this is! Think of the unrest and agitation in the world today—all because men reject true Wisdom and act according to their own supposed cleverness!

THE CHARACTER OF TRUE WISDOM (3:17-18)

True wisdom is described in verse 17. The Lord Jesus is here! The wisdom that comes from God is first pure. In thought, word and deed, it is clean. In spirit and body, in doctrine and practice, in faith and in morals, it is undefiled. It is also peaceable. This simply means that a wise man loves peace, and he will do all he can to maintain peace without sacrificing purity. This is illustrated by Luther's story of the two goats that met on a narrow bridge over deep water. They could not go back and they did not dare to fight. "After a short parley, one of them lay down and let the other go over him, and thus no harm was done. The moral," Luther would say, "is easy: be content if thy person is trod upon for peace's sake; thy person, I say, not thy conscience." True wisdom is gentle. It is forbearing, not overbearing: courteous, not crude. A wise man is a gentleman, respectful of the feelings of others. Says A. B. Simpson, "The rude, sarcastic manner, the sharp retort, the unkind cut—all these have nothing whatever in common with the gentle teaching of the Comforter."

The next characteristic is *easy to be entreated*. It means conciliatory, approachable, open to reason, ready to yield when truth requires it. It is the opposite of obstinate and adamant. Wisdom from above is full of mercy and good fruits. It is full of mercy to those who are in the wrong, and anxious to help them find the right way. It is compassionate and kind. There is no vindictiveness in it; indeed, it rewards discourtesy with benevolence. It is without partiality, that is, it does not practice favoritism. It is impartial in its treatment of others. Finally, true wisdom is without hypocrisy. It is sincere and genuine. It does not pretend to be other than it actually is.

Now let us put all these thoughts together to form the portraits of two men—the truly wise man and the man with false wisdom.

PORTRAIT OF MR. TRULY WISE

The man who is truly wise is truly humble. He estimates others to be better than himself. He does not put on airs, but does put others at ease right away.

His behavior is not like that of the world around him; it is otherworldly. He does not live for the body but for the spirit. In words and deeds, he makes you think of the Lord Jesus. His life is pure. Morally and spiritually he is clean. Then too he is peaceable. He will endure insult and false accusation but he will not fight back or even seek to justify himself. He is a gentle person, mild-mannered and tenderhearted. And he is easy to reason with, willing to try to see the other person's viewpoint. He is not vindictive but always ready to forgive those who have wronged him. Not only so but he habitually shows kindness to others, especially those who don't deserve it. And he is the same to all; he doesn't play favorites. The rich receive the same treatment as the poor; the great are not preferred above the common people. Finally, he is not a hypocrite. He doesn't say one thing and mean another. You will never hear him flatter. He speaks the truth and never wears a mask.

PORTRAIT OF MR. WORLDLY-WISE

The worldly-wise man is not so. His heart is filled with envy and strife. In his determination to enrich himself, he becomes intolerant of every rival or competitor. There is nothing noble about his behavior; it rises no higher than this earth. He lives to gratify his natural appetites—just as the animals do. And his methods are cruel, treacherous, and devilish. Beneath his well pressed suit is a life of impurity. His thought life is polluted. His morals are debased. His speech is unclean. He is quarrelsome with all who disagree with him or who cross him in any way. At home, at work, in social life, he is constantly contentious. And he is harsh and overbearing, rude and crude. People cannot approach him easily; he keeps them at arm's length. To reason with him quietly is all but impossible. His mind is already made up, and his opinions are not subject to change. He is unforgiving and vindictive. When he catches someone in a fault or error, he shows no mercy. Rather he unleashes a torrent of abuse, discourtesy and meanness. He values people according to the benefit they might be to him. When he can no longer "use" them, that is, when there is no further hope of profit from knowing them, he loses interest in them. Finally, he is two-faced and insincere. You can never be sure of him—either of his words or actions.

A FINAL PICTURE

James closes the chapter with the words, "And the fruit of righteousness is sown in peace of them that make peace" (verse 18). This verse is a connecting link between what we have been discussing and what is to follow. We have just learned that true wisdom is peace-loving. In the next chapter we find conflict among God's people. Here we are reminded that life is like the farming process. We have the farmer (the wise man who is a peace maker); the climate (peace) and the harvest (righteousness). The farmer wants to raise a harvest of righteousness. Can this be done in an atmosphere of quarrels and bickering? No, the sowing must take place under peaceful conditions. It must be done by those who are of a peaceful disposition. A harvest of uprightness will be produced in their own lives and in the lives of those to whom they minister.

"And the wise are peacemakers who go on quietly sowing for a harvest of righteousness—in other people and in themselves" (verse 18, Phillips).

Once again James has put our faith on trial, this time with regard to the type of wisdom which we manifest in our everyday life. We must ask ourselves—Do I respect the proud men of the world more than the humble believer in the Lord Jesus? Do I serve the Lord without caring who gets the credit? Do I sometimes use questionable means in order to get good results? Am I guilty of flattery in order to influence people? Do I harbor jealousy and resentment in my heart? Do I resort to sarcasm and unkind remarks? Am I pure in thought, in speech, in morals?

When you are ready, complete Exam 3 by answering questions 11-20 on pages 63-64. (You should have already answered questions 1-10 as part of your study of lesson 5.)

THE EPISTLE OF JAMES

Exam

Name _____ Grade _____

(print plainly)

Address _____

Zip   Class

City _____ State _____ Code _____ Number _____

Instructor _____

LESSON 5

In the blank space in the right-hand margin write the letter of the correct answer.

1. James tells us that
   a. no one should want to teach
   b. everyone should have a strong ambition to teach God's Word
   c. a Bible teaching ministry should not be undertaken lightly
   d. so long as the teacher's motives, methods and messages are right that's all that matters   *A*

2. The true test of whether or not a man has truly "arrived" (i.e., become "perfect") in his Christian life is in how
   a. many souls he has won for the Lord
   b. well he has mastered the Scriptures
   c. quickly he can receive answers to prayer
   d. well he can control his tongue   *A*

3. James likens the tongue to a horse's
   a. collar
   b. saddle
   c. reigns
   d. bit   *D*

4. Which of the following is used by James as an illustration of the tongue's power to spread damage? A
   a. plague
   b. fire
   c. flood
   d. famine   *B*

5. When a person spreads gossip he
a. defiles himself
b. enhances his own image as a conversationalist
c. gives the person to whom he speaks a fair picture of the person about whom he speaks
d. sets in motion forces over which he has complete control

A

6. The tongue sets on fire "the course of nature." That is, it sets on fire the
a. forces of nature
b. resources of nature
c. beauty of nature
d. wheel of nature

A

7. The "course of nature" is a reference to the
a. whole round of human activity
b. secret spirit powers which are behind natural events
c. time element in human life
d. four seasons

B

8. Speaking of the tongue as being "full of deadly poison," James is doubtless thinking of
a. a serpent
b. a deadly drug
c. an unwholesome plant
d. an uncleansed wound

A

9. To overcome the sin of evil speaking one should
a. ask for the Lord's help daily
b. refuse to speak unfavorably about anyone
c. endeavor to look for the good in other people
d. do all the above

D

10. When speaking of good and evil fruit and of salt and fresh water, James is teaching us that
a. it is impossible for a truly saved person to speak ill of anyone
b. an unsaved person cannot speak good of anyone
c. only a person with a split personality can use his tongue to say both good things and evil things
d. our speech ought to be consistently good

A

WHAT DO YOU SAY?

What steps have you taken to get victory over sins of the tongue?

_____

_____

_____

_____

_____

LESSON 6

In the blank space in the right-hand margin write the letter of the correct answer.

11. When speaking of wisdom, James means
   a. the amount of knowledge we have acquired
   b. our reputation
   c. our scholastic achievements
   d. our application to life of the knowledge we have   *D*

12. The only truly wise man was
   a. the Lord Jesus
   b. Solomon
   c. Confucius
   d. Moses   *A*

13. Which of the following is an *essential* characteristic of true
   wisdom?
   a. happiness
   b. humility
   c. hospitality
   d. cleverness   *B*

14. The worldly-wise man will
   a. always be a success in this life
   b. never be a success in this life
   c. be a jealous man
   d. usually refrain from boasting   *B*

15. James says that false wisdom is
   a. clever, cunning and confident
   b. earthly, sensual and devilish
   c. philosophical, religious and scientific
   d. candid, cruel and contentious

B

16. When James says of true wisdom that it is "peaceable" he
   a. is speaking parabolically
   b. advocates surrendering on every issue no matter what it is
   c. means that the wise man will go to great lengths to secure peace
   d. shows how impractical it is to try to employ this kind of wisdom in today's world

A

17. A wise man confronted with someone who is in the wrong will
   a. talk about him
   b. argue with him
   c. ignore him
   d. seek to help him

D

18. Turn to Genesis 25:28. Isaac and Rebekah revealed lack of true wisdom by
   a. telling lies
   b. stubbornness
   c. discourtesy
   d. having favorites

D

19. Read the story of Nabal in 1 Samuel 25. This man lacked true wisdom. His "wisdom" revealed itself in his character. He
   a. was abusive, discourteous and mean
   b. could not be approached easily
   c. was quarrelsome and cross
   d. all the above

D

20. James likens life to
   a. farming
   b. fishing
   c. flying
   d. feasting

D

64

WHAT DO YOU SAY?

How would you react to someone who gossiped about you?

_____

_____

_____

_____

_____

Lesson 7

Covetousness   (James 4:1-5)

James has just pointed out that the wise man is a peace-loving man. Now he is reminded of the tragic strife that often exists among God's people. What is the cause of it all? Why are there so many unhappy homes and so many assemblies torn by division? Why are there such bitter feuds among Christian workers in the homeland, and such conflicts among missionaries abroad? The reason is that we are ceaselessly striving to satisfy our lust for pleasures and possessions, and to outdo others.

THE SOURCE OF ALL OUR SQUABBLES (4:1-2a)

The sad fact is that there *are* wars and battles among Christians. To suggest that this paragraph does not apply to believers is unrealistic, and it robs the passage of all its value for us. What causes all this fighting? It arises from the strong desires within us which are constantly struggling to be satisfied (verse 1). There is the lust to accumulate material possessions. There is the drive for prestige. There is the craving for pleasure, for the gratification of bodily appetites. These powerful forces are at work within us. We are never satisfied. We always want more. And yet it seems we are constantly frustrated in our desire to get what we want. The unfulfilled longing becomes so powerful that we trample on those who seem to obstruct our progress. James says, "Ye kill." Of course, he uses the word in a figurative sense. We don't literally kill, but the anger, jealousy and cruelty which we generate are murder in embryo (verse 2a).

WHY WE ARE NEVER SATISFIED (4:2b-3)

We covet and cannot obtain. We want to have more things and better things than others. And in the attempt, we find ourselves quarreling and devouring one another.

John and Jane have just been married. John has a fair job with a moderate salary. Jane wants a house as good as the other young couples at church. John wants a late model car. Jane wants fine furnishings and appliances. Some of these things have to be purchased on the installment plan. John's salary is hardly sufficient to bear the strain. Then a baby is born into the family; this means added expenses and a badly unbalanced budget. As Jane's demands mount, John becomes cross and irritable. Jane retaliates with backbiting and tears. Soon the walls of the house are vibrating with the cross-fire. Materialism is destroying the home.

On the other hand, it may be that Jane is jealous. She feels that Bob and Sue Smith have a more prominent place in the assembly than she and John. Soon she makes snide remarks to Sue. As the battle between them increases in tempo, John and Bob become involved in the fighting. Then the other Christians take sides, and the assembly is divided—because of one person's lust for prominence.

Here then is the source of the bickering and strife among believers. It comes from the desire for more, and from jealousy of others. "Keeping up with the Joneses" is a polite name for it; more accurately we should call it greed, covetousness and envy. The desire becomes so strong that people will do almost anything to gratify their lusts. They are slow to learn that true pleasure is not found in this way, but in contentment with food and raiment (1 Timothy 6:8).

Prayer is the right approach to this problem. "Don't argue. Don't fight. Pray." James says, "Ye have not, because ye ask not." Instead of taking these things to the Lord in prayer, we try to get what we want by our own efforts. If we want something which we do not have,

68

we should ask God for it. If we do ask, and the prayer is unanswered, what then? It simply means that our motives were not pure (verse 3). We did not want these possessions for the glory of God or for the good of our fellow men. We wanted them for our own selfish enjoyment. We wanted them to satisfy our natural appetites. God does not promise to answer such prayers.

What a profound lesson in psychology we have in these first three verses! If men were content with what God has given them, what staggering conflict and unrest would be avoided! If we loved our neighbors as ourselves, and were more interested in sharing than in acquiring, what peace would result! If we would follow the Savior's command to forsake all instead of to accumulate, to lay up treasures in heaven rather than on earth, what contentions would cease!

COVETOUSNESS REBUKED (4:4-5)

In verse 4, James condemns the inordinate love of material things as spiritual adultery. God wants us to love Him first and foremost. When we love the passing things of this world, we are being untrue to Him. We are adulteresses (note that only the feminine form of the word is used in the ASV and most other versions).

Covetousness is a form of idolatry. It means that we strongly desire what God does not want us to have. That means that we have set up idols in our hearts. We value material things above the will of God. Therefore, covetousness is idolatry, and idolatry is spiritual unfaithfulness to the Lord.

Worldliness is also enmity against God. The world, in verse 4, does not mean the planet on which we live, or the world of nature about us. It is the system which man has built up for himself in an effort to satisfy the lust of the eyes, the lust of the flesh and the pride of life. In this system there is no room for God or for His Son. It may be the world of art, of culture, of education, of science or even of religion. But it is a sphere in which the Name of Christ is unwelcome or even forbidden, except, of course, as an empty formality. It is, in short, the world of mankind outside the sphere of the church. To be a friend of this system is to be an enemy of God. It was this world that crucified the Lord of life and glory. In fact, it was the *religious* world that played the key role in putting Him to death. How unthinkable it is that believers should ever want to walk arm-in-arm with the world that murdered their Savior!

Verse 5 is one of the most difficult in the epistle: "Do ye think that the scripture saith in vain, The spirit that dwelleth in us lusteth to envy?"

The first difficulty is that James seems to be quoting a verse from the Old Testament; yet these words are not found anywhere in the Old Testament, or even in the Apocryphal books. There are two possible explanations. First of all, while the exact words are not found in the Old Testament, James may have been quoting them as being the general teaching of the Scripture. The second solution of the problem is given by the Revised Version. There the verse is broken into two questions: "Or think ye that the scripture speaketh in vain? Doth the spirit which he made to dwell in us long unto envying?" Here the thought is that in condemning the competitive, worldly spirit, the Bible is not wasting words.

The second major difficulty in verse 5 is the meaning of the second part of the verse. The problem, of course, is whether the spirit is the Holy Spirit or the spirit of passionate jealousy. If the former is meant, then the thought is that the Holy Spirit which God made to dwell in us does not originate the lust and jealousy which cause strife; rather He yearns over us with jealousy for our entire devotion to Christ. If the latter is intended, then the meaning is that the spirit that dwells in us, that is, the spirit of lust and envy, is the cause of all our unfaithfulness to God.

When you have mastered this lesson, take the first part of Exam 4 (covering lesson 7), questions 1-10 on pages 77-78 (right after lesson 8).

Lesson 8

Help From Above (James 4:6-17)

"But He giveth more grace" (verse 6). In the first five verses we saw how wicked the old nature of the believer can be. Now we learn that we are not left to deal with the lusts of the flesh in our own strength.

GRACE FOR EVERY NEED (4:6)

Thank God, He gives grace or strength whenever it is needed (Hebrews 4:16). He has promised, " . . . as thy days, so shall thy strength be" (Deuteronomy 33:25).

> He giveth more grace when the burdens grow greater,
> He sendeth more strength when the labors increase,
> To added affliction He addeth His mercy,
> To multiplied trials His multiplied peace.

To prove that God gives grace as it is needed, James quotes Proverbs 3:34, but here there is the added thought that it is to the humble, not the proud, that this grace is promised. God resists the proud, but He cannot resist the broken spirit.

TRUE REPENTANCE (4:7-10)

In verses 7-10, we find six steps to be followed where there is true repentance. James has been crying out against sins of the saints. His words have pierced our hearts like arrows of conviction. They have fallen like thunderbolts from the throne of God. We realize that God has been speaking to us. Our hearts have been bowed beneath the influence of His Word. But the question now is, "What shall we do?"

The first thing to do is to *submit to God* (verse 7a). This means that we must be subject to Him, ready to listen to Him and to obey Him. We must be tender and contrite, not proud and stiff-necked. Then we must *resist the devil* (verse 7b). We do this by closing our ears and hearts to his suggestions and temptations. We do it also by using the Scriptures as the Sword of the Spirit to repel him. If we resist him, he will flee from us. Next we should *draw nigh to God* (verse 8). We do this by prayer. We must come before Him in desperate, believing prayer, telling Him all that is on our heart. As we thus approach Him, we find that He draws near to us. We thought He would be far from us because of our carnality and worldliness, but when we draw near to Him, He forgives us and restores us. The fourth step is: "*Cleanse your hands,* ye sinners; and *purify your hearts*, ye double minded." The hands speak of our actions and the heart represents our motives and desires. We cleanse our hands and purify our hearts through confession and forsaking of sins, both outward and inward. As sinners we need to confess evil acts; as double minded people we need to confess our mixed motives. Confession should be accompanied by *deep sorrow for sin* (verse 9). "Be afflicted, and mourn, and weep: let your laughter be turned to mourning, and your joy to heaviness." When God visits us in conviction of sin, it is no time for levity. Rather it is a time when we should prostrate ourselves before Him and mourn over our sinfulness, powerlessness, coldness and barrenness. We should humble ourselves and weep over our materialism, secularism and formalism. Both inwardly and outwardly, we should manifest the fruit of godly repentance. Finally, we should *humble ourselves in the sight of the Lord.* If we honestly take our place in the dust at His feet, He will exalt us in due time.

This then is the way we should respond when the Lord exposes us to ourselves. Too often it is not the case, however. Sometimes, for example, we are in a meeting when God speaks loudly to our hearts.

We are stirred for the moment, and filled with good resolves. But when the meeting closes, the people engage in animated and light-hearted conversation. The whole atmosphere of the meeting is dispersed, the power is dissipated, and the Spirit of God is quenched.

THE SIN OF EVIL SPEAKING (4:11-12)

The next sin which James deals with (verses 11, 12) is that of censoriousness, or speaking evil against a brother. Someone has suggested that there are three questions we should answer before indulging in criticism of others—What good does it do your brother? What good does it do yourself? What glory for God is in it?

Beth Day has expressed it as follows in her poem "Three Gates of Gold."

> . . . Make it pass
> Before you speak, three gates of gold:
> These narrow gates. First "Is it true?"
> Then "Is it needful?" In your mind
> Give truthful answer. And the next
> Is last and narrowest, "Is it kind?"
> And if to reach your lips at last
> It passed through these gateways three,
> Then you may tell the tale, nor fear
> What the result of speech may be.

The royal law of love says that we should love our neighbor as ourselves. To speak evil against a brother, therefore, or to judge his motives, is the same as speaking against this law and condemning it as worthless (verse 11). To break a law deliberately is to treat it with disrespect and contempt. It is the same as saying that the law is not good, and not worthy of obedience. "He who refuses obedience virtually says it ought not to be law." Now this puts the one who speaks evil against his brother in the strange position of being a judge rather than one who is to be judged (verse 12). He sets himself up as being superior to the law rather than subject to it. But only God is superior to the law; He is the One who gave it and the One who judges by it. Who then has the audacity to usurp the place of God by speaking maliciously against a brother?

THE SIN OF SELF-CONFIDENCE (4:13-17)

The next sin which James denounces is that of self-confidence, of boastful planning in independence of God (verses 13-16). He pictures a businessman who has a complete plan laid out for the future. Notice the details. He thought about the time (today or tomorrow); the personnel (we); the place (this city); the duration (spend a year there); the activity (trade) and the anticipated result (get gain). What is missing in this picture? He never once takes God into his business. In life, it is necessary to make some plans for the future, but to do so in self-will is sinful. To say "we will" or "I will" is the essence of sin. Note, for instance, the "I wills" of Lucifer in Isaiah 14:13, 14, "For thou hast said in thine heart, I will ascend into heaven, I will exalt my throne above the stars of God: I will sit also upon the mount of the congregation, in the sides of the north: I will ascend above the heights of the clouds; I will be like the most High."

It is wrong to plan as if tomorrow were certain. "Say not . . . tomorrow" (Proverbs 3:28). We do not know what tomorrow holds. Our lives are as frail and unpredictable as a "puff of smoke" (Phillips). God should be consulted in all our plans, and they should be made in His will (verse 15). We should live and speak in the realization that our destinies are in His control. We should say, "If the Lord will, we shall both live and do this and that." Thus, in the book of Acts, we find the Apostle Paul saying, " . . . I will return again unto you, *if God will*" (18:21), and in 1 Corinthians 4:19, he wrote, "But I will come to you shortly, *if the Lord will*. . . ." Sometimes Christians employ the letters D.V. to express this sense of dependence on God. These letters are the initials of two Latin words, *Deo volente*, meaning *God willing*.

"But now you glory in your vauntings," says James (verse 16). The Christians were priding themselves in their boastful plans for the future. They were arrogant in their confidence that nothing would interfere with their time schedule. They acted as if they were the masters of their own fate. All such boasting is sinful because it leaves God out.

"Therefore to him that knoweth to do good, and doeth it not, to him it is sin" (verse 17). To do good, in this context, is to take God into every aspect of our lives, to live in moment by moment dependence on Him. If we know we should do this, yet fail to do it, we are clearly sinning. Of course, the principle is of broader application. In any area of life, the opportunity to do good makes us responsible to do it. If we know what is right, we are under obligation to live up to that light. Failure to do so involves us in sin against God, against our neighbors and against ourselves.

In chapter 4, James has put us on trial with regard to covetousness and conflict, with regard to evil-speaking and with regard to planning without consulting the Lord. Let us therefore ask ourselves the following questions—Am I continually anxious to get more or am I content with what I have? Am I envious of those who have more than I? Do I pray before purchasing? When God speaks to me do I submit or resist? Do I speak against my brothers? Do I make plans without consulting the Lord?

When you are ready, complete Exam 4 by answering questions 11-20 on pages 79-80. (You should have already answered questions 1-10 as part of your study of lesson 7.)

Name_____ Exam Grade_____
(print plainly)

Address _____

City _____ State _____ Zip Code _____ Class Number _____

Instructor _____

LESSON 7

In the blank space in the right-hand margin write the letter of the correct answer.

1. The *introduction* to the section on covetousness in James' epistle is found in what James has to say about
a. materialism
b. wisdom
c. self-discipline
d. idolatry

B

2. The section on squabbles in James' epistle
a. cannot possibly apply to Christians
b. certainly does apply to Christians
c. is a later addition to the text inserted by a scribe more knowledgeable about human nature than James
d. was inspired by discords in James' own domestic circle

B

3. Many fights are caused by
a. the desire for material possessions
b. the lust for prestige
c. the craving for pleasure
d. all the above

D

4. When James says "Ye kill" he
a. is addressing himself to the unsaved only
b. is speaking to Christians but is speaking symbolically
c. is speaking to Christians and means that some of the ones he knew had actually committed murder
d. was speaking only to Christians of his day when killing was not considered a capital crime

B

5. Which of the following is "murder in embryo" as James means it?
   a. Using birth control devices
   b. Desiring to be promoted at work
   c. Generating anger
   d. Neglecting to help the sick

C

6. The solution to strife which James advocates is
   a. prayer
   b. toleration
   c. separation from contentious Christians
   d. stronger church discipline

A

7. According to James the reason why many prayers remain unanswered is that the requests are
   a. not prayed in the right words
   b. not asked in the Name of the Lord Jesus
   c. made by unsaved people
   d. made from impure motives

D

8. James says that a love for this world is
   a. sometimes acceptable
   b. spiritual adultery
   c. quite natural
   d. never really wrong

B

9. When James speaks of "the world" he is referring to
   a. the world of nature
   b. the planet on which we live
   c. human life and society with God left out
   d. the entire solar system

C

10. Turn to Matthew 20:20-24. This squabble the disciples had among themselves resulted from a lust for
   a. pleasure
   b. possessions
   c. position
   d. popularity

C

WHAT DO YOU SAY?

What was the cause of your last squabble?

_____

_____

_____

_____

_____

LESSON 8

In the blank space in the right-hand margin write the letter of the correct answer.

11. James quotes Proverbs 3:34 to show that
a. God gives grace to all men
b. God's grace is very limited
c. grace from God is bestowed on the humble
d. saving grace is different from sanctifying grace

12. The first step in spiritual restoration and victory is to
a. resist the devil
b. submit to God
c. resolve to do better next time
d. try harder to be good

13. When James says "cleanse your hands" he is
a. referrring to our actions
b. saying that "cleanliness (of the body) is next to godliness"
c. advocating ritualistic "washings" as part of Christian worship
d. expecting us to take him literally

14. Confession should be accompanied by
a. acts of penance
b. mourning and sorrow for sin
c. vows of chastity and resolves to do better next time
d. peace offerings in the form of donations to charity to ensure a hearing from God

79

15. Before criticizing someone we ought to ask ourselves
    a. "What good will it do?"
    b. "Will it help me spiritually?"
    c. "How will it bring glory to God?"
    d. all the above questions

    D

16. The "royal law" says we should
    a. honor the king
    b. worship God
    c. submit to civil government
    d. love our neighbor as ourselves

    A

17. To break a law deliberately is to
    a. assert one's rights
    b. show contempt for that law
    c. aid in the repeal of that law
    d. prove we are not under law but under grace

    B

18. All planning for the future
    a. is foolish, to say the least
    b. makes us like Lucifer
    c. should be done subject to God's will
    d. is condemned by Scripture

    C

19. James says that if we know what is the proper thing to do
    but fail to do it we
    a. are guilty of sin
    b. set others a poor example
    c. can be excused under certain circumstances
    d. should be ashamed of ourselves

    A

20. Read Luke 12:16-20. The man in the story was guilty of
    a. speaking evil of a brother
    b. breaking the commandment forbidding stealing
    c. leaving God out of his plans
    d. trying to earn his salvation by works instead of accepting
       it through grace

    C

WHAT DO YOU SAY?

Describe a victory God has given you over Satan.

_____

_____

_____

_____

_____

Lesson 9

The Woes of the Wealthy (James 5:1-6)

In one of the most searching and piercing sections of his letter, James now launches into a denunciation of the sins of the rich. The words fall like hammer-blows, blunt and unsparing. In fact, the denunciation is so strong that these verses are seldom preached on.

James is here seen in the role of a prophet of social justice. He cries out against the failure of the rich to use their money for the alleviation of human need. He condemns those who have become rich by exploiting their workers. He rebukes their use of wealth for self-indulgence and luxurious living. Finally, he pictures the rich as arrogant oppressors of the righteous.

A PROPHETIC WORD (5:1)

First he summons the rich men to weep and moan because of the miseries which they were about to experience. Soon they would meet God. Then they would be filled with shame and remorse. They would see that they had been unfaithful stewards. They would wail over the opportunities they had missed. They would mourn over their covetousness and selfishness. They would be convicted about their unfair employment practices. They would see the sin of seeking security in material things rather than in the Lord. And they would shed hot tears over the way in which they had indulged themselves to the full.

FOUR SINS OF THE RICH (5:2-6)

James mentions four cardinal sins of the rich. The first is the sin of hoarding wealth.

1. Laying up Treasures on Earth (5:2-3)

"Your richest goods are ruined," says James, "your hoard of clothes is moth-eaten; your gold and silver are tarnished. Yes, their very tarnish will be the evidence of your wicked hoarding and you will shrink from them as if they were red-hot" (Phillips).

The Bible never says that it is a sin to be rich. A person, for instance, may inherit a fortune overnight and certainly he has not committed any sin in thus becoming rich. But the Bible does teach that it is wrong to hoard riches. The Lord Jesus expressly forbade the hoarding of wealth. He said, "Lay not up for yourselves treasures upon earth, where moth and rust doth corrupt, and where thieves break through and steal: but lay up for yourselves treasures in heaven, where neither moth nor rust doth corrupt, and where thieves do not break through nor steal: for where your treasure is, there will your heart be also" (Matthew 6:19-21).

James speaks of wealth in four forms: riches, garments, gold and silver. In Bible times, wealth was generally in the form of: grain, oil, and other produce; clothing, gold, or silver. Perhaps when James says, "Your riches are corrupted . . . ," he means that the grain had become wormy and the oil had become rancid. The point is that these things had been hoarded to the point where they were spoiled. They could have been used at one time to feed the hungry; now they were worthless. "Your garments are become moth-eaten," he says. This doesn't happen to clothing that is in regular use. But when the closet is so crowded with garments that they are used very infrequently, they are subject to moth damage. To James it is morally wrong to hoard clothes like this when so many people in the world are in desperate need. "Your gold and silver is cankered; and the rust of them shall be a witness against you, and shall eat your flesh as it were fire," he continues. We know that gold and silver do not rust, but they do tarnish and become discolored, and under unfavorable storage conditions, they could conceivably corrode. Instead of putting their money to work, feeding the hungry, clothing the destitute, providing medicines for the sick, and spreading the gospel, the rich were saving their money for a "rainy day." It benefited no one, and eventually rotted away.

The rust, speaking of disuse and decay, will be a condemning testimony against the rich. If this was true of the rich people of James' day, how much more true is it of believers in our day? What will be our condemnation if we have had the means of spreading the gospel and have failed to use it? If we have hoarded material things when they might have been used in the salvation of souls? The expression "the rust . . . shall eat your flesh as it were fire" means that their failure to use their riches for the good of others would cause them the keenest suffering and remorse. When their eyes would at last be opened to see the cruelty of their selfishness and greed (costly jewelry, elegant clothing, luxurious homes, high-priced cars), it would be a scalding, scorching experience.

2.   Failure to Pay Proper Wages (5:4)

The second sin which James attacks is the acquisition of wealth by failure to pay proper wages. Those who mowed the fields were deprived of their rightful pay. Though the workers might protest, they were quite helpless to get redress. They had no one on earth to plead their cause successfully. However, their cries were heard by the Lord of Sabaoth, that is, the Lord of hosts. He who commands the armies of heaven is strong in behalf of earth's downtrodden masses. The Lord God Omnipotent will help and avenge them. Thus, the Bible condemns not only the hoarding of wealth but the acquisition of wealth by dishonest means. In addition to the sin of paying inadequate wages, James could also have mentioned falsifying income tax returns, cheating on weights and measures, bribing local inspectors or other officials, false advertising and falsifying expense accounts.

3. Luxurious Living (5:5)

Next James denounces the luxurious living of the rich. Expensive jewelry, elegant clothes, epicurean foods and palatial homes—how could they squander their wealth on self when multitudes were in desperate need? Or to bring it down to our own day, how can we justify the affluence and extravagance of the church and of Christian people? We live in a world where thousands die daily of starvation. Over half the world's population have never heard of the Lord Jesus Christ. In such a world, how can we justify our magnificent churches and chapels? How can we justify our sports cars, limousines, speed boats? How can we spend the Lord's money in expensive hotels, in high-class restaurants, in any form of self-indulgence? The clear teaching of the Scriptures, the appalling need of the world, the example of the Savior and the simple instinct of compassion tell us that it is wrong to live in comfort, luxury and ease as long as there is a single soul who has not heard the gospel.

Those who live in pleasure and who are "wanton," that is, unrestrained in luxury, are likened to those who nourish their hearts in a day of slaughter—like animals, fattening themselves just before their execution, or like soldiers who spend their time looting when others are perishing around them.

4. Inhumanity Towards the Righteous (5:6)

The final charge against the rich is that they condemned and killed the righteous one, and he didn't resist them. Some think that the righteous one is the Lord Jesus. However, His death was brought about by the religious rather than by the rich. It is probably best to think of "the righteous one" as representing innocent men in general. James is thinking of the rough, high-handed way in which rich people have characteristically behaved toward their subordinates. They have condemned them by false accusation, by harsh language and by threats. They have killed them, not directly perhaps, but by overworking and underpaying them. The innocent offered no resistance. To protest might result in further brutality, or dismissal from his job.

When you have mastered this lesson, take the first part of Exam 5 (covering lesson 9), questions 1-10 on pages 93-94 (right after lesson 10).

Lesson 10

Patience Please (James 5:7-12)

James now turns to the believers who were being oppressed, and encourages them to be patient.

JESUS IS COMING SOON (5:7-8)

The motive for patience is the coming of the Lord. This may refer either to the Rapture or to Christ's coming to reign. Both are used in the New Testament as incentives to patient endurance.

The farmer illustrates the need of patience (verse 7). He does not reap on the same day that he plants. Rather there is a long period of waiting. First there must come the early rain, causing the seed to germinate. Then at the end of the season is the latter rain, needed to bring the crop to successful fruition. Some see in this reference to early and latter rain a promise that the blessings of Pentecost at the beginning of the church age will be repeated before the Lord's return, but the overall tenor of New Testament Scripture seems to discourage such an expectation. However, there is nothing to forbid our looking for a faithful remnant of believers on fire for God and bent on world evangelization. What better way to welcome the returning Savior?

The wrongs of earth will be made right when the Lord returns. Therefore His people should be patient, like the farmer. Their hearts should be established with the certainty of His coming (verse 8).

DON'T GRUMBLE (5:9)

During times of persecution and distress, it is not uncommon for the victims to turn against one another. It is a curious twist of human nature that in times of pressure we build up wrath against those we love most. Hence the warning, "Grudge (murmur) ye not one against another, brethren, lest ye be condemned." The word *grudge* here does not mean to allow reluctantly but rather to have inward resentments that are unexpressed. This verse has a voice for servants of the Lord working together under trying circumstances. We should not let resentment build up. After all, the Judge is already at the door. He knows what we think. Soon we will stand before the Judgment Seat of Christ to give an account. We should not judge lest we be judged.

SOME EXAMPLES (5:10-11)

The Old Testament prophets are brought forth as examples of sufferings and patience (ASV). Note that sufferings precede patience. "Tribulation worketh patience" (Romans 5:3). Trouble produces endurance. As explained previously, patience in the New Testament means fortitude or steadfastness. Because of their faithfulness in declaring the word of the Lord, the prophets were persecuted unmercifully. Yet they endured as seeing Him who is invisible (Hebrews 11:27). See also Hebrews 11: 32-40.

We look back upon prophets such as Isaiah, Jeremiah and Daniel with a great deal of respect. We honor them for their lives of zeal and devotion. In this sense we call them "blessed." We agree that they were right and the world was wrong. Well, we should remember that they went through great trials and sufferings, and that they endured with patience. If we want to be blessed, it is only reasonable to conclude that we will be called upon to do the same.

Job is a fine example of endurance or fortitude. Few if any men in the history of the world have ever suffered so much loss in so short a time as Job. Yet he never cursed God, or turned from Him. In the end, his endurance was rewarded. God revealed Himself, as He always does, to be merciful and full of pity.

If we did not know what James calls "the end of the Lord" (that is the final issue or result which the Lord brings to pass), we might be tempted to envy the wicked. Asaph was jealous when he saw the prosperity of the wicked (Psalm 73:3-17). The more he thought about it, the more perturbed he became. Then he went into the sanctuary of God and understood their latter end. This dispelled all his envy. David had the same experience. In Psalm 17:14 he describes the portion of the ungodly in this life, then in the next verse contrasts the portion of the believer in the life to come. In view of this, it pays the believer to be steadfast. In Job's case, "the end of the Lord" was that God gave him twice as much as he had before (Job 42:10-15).

DON'T SWEAR (5:12)

Impatience in times of trial is also manifested in swearing. Here it is not a question of profanity, or cursing, primarily. Neither is it a matter of taking an oath in a court of law. The practice forbidden is the thoughtless use of the Lord's Name or some other name to attest the truthfulness of one's speech. The Christian should not have to swear by anyone or anything, either in heaven or on earth. Those who know him should be able to depend on the fact that his yes means yes and his no means no.

Of course, this passage could also be applied to forbid such needless expressions as "For heaven's sake," "As God is my Judge," "By Jove" and such minced oaths as "gee" (contraction for Jesus), "gosh" and "golly" (slang for God).

"Lest you fall into condemnation," says James, perhaps thinking of the third commandment: "Thou shalt not take the name of the Lord thy God in vain; for the Lord will not hold him guiltless that taketh His name in vain" (Exodus 20:7).

Complete Exam 5 by answering questions 11-20.

Name _____

(print plainly)

Exam
Grade _____

Address _____

City _____ State _____

Zip
Code _____

Class
Number _____

Instructor _____

LESSON 9

In the blank space in the right-hand margin write the letter of the correct answer.

1. James assumes the role of
   a. an ordained minister
   b. a penniless beggar
   c. a prophet of social justice
   d. a wealthy land owner

   C _____

2. James tells the rich to weep because
   a. they are soon to meet God
   b. inflation will eat up their profits
   c. capitalism is inherently evil
   d. no man can serve two masters

   D _____

3. The Bible says that
   a. money is the root of all evil
   b. it is a sin to be rich
   c. only the poor can be truly saved
   d. riches must not be hoarded

   D _____

4. Putting money aside for "a rainy day" is seen by James as
   a. an excellent idea
   b. a misuse of one's resources
   c. a matter of personal conviction
   d. consistent with a life of faith

   B _____

93

5. James finds fault with which of the following methods of gaining wealth? Becoming rich
   a. at the expense of others
   b. by buying and selling real estate
   c. through the receipt of an inheritance
   d. in all the above ways

   A

6. The name by which God associates Himself with the down-trodden masses is the name
   a. Elohim
   b. The Lord of Hosts
   c. Jehovah Jireh ("the Lord will provide")
   d. The Almighty

   C

7. James says that those who live in pleasure on the earth are
   a. weak
   b. wayward
   c. wanton
   d. wise

   C

8. When James says of the rich that they are guilty of condemning and killing "the righteous one" he is probably thinking of
   a. the Lord Jesus
   b. the martyr Stephen
   c. James the disciple
   d. innocent men in general

   A

9. Read Acts 4:34-37. What did Barnabas do with his property? He
   a. sold it and gave the proceeds to the Lord's work
   b. sold it and gave the Lord ten per cent of his capital gain
   c. invested it and gave the income it produced to the church
   d. used the income it brought in as a means of supporting himself in the Lord's work

   A

10. Which of the following was snared by money? (Look up the references.)
    a. The ruler (Luke 18:18-23)
    b. Gehazi (2 Kings 5:1-27)
    c. The man with five brothers (Luke 16:19-31)
    d. All of the above

    D

94

WHAT DO YOU SAY?

How has God spoken to you in this lesson?

_____

_____

_____

_____

_____

LESSON 10

In the blank space in the right-hand margin write the letter of the correct answer.

11. The motive for patience is
    a. the Great White Throne
    b. God's sovereignty over our circumstances
    c. the hope that our bad luck will change
    d. the Lord's return

12. James cites which of the following as an example of patience?
    The
    a. father
    b. fisherman
    c. farmer
    d. financier

13. To take James' reference to "the latter rain" as a promise of a
    second Pentecost at the end of the Church age is
    a. certainly correct
    b. certainly wrong
    c. probably correct
    d. probably unjustified

14. James warns against having inward resentments against other
    Christians on the ground that
    a. nobody is perfect
    b. the Lord is at the door
    c. such attitudes usually backfire
    d. no truly saved person can harbor a grudge

15. To which of the following does James point as examples of patient endurance? The

a. patriarchs of the Old Testament

b. prophets of the Old Testament

c. Lord Jesus Himself

d. the New Testament apostles

A

16. Read Job 1:6 - 2:13. Which of the following did Job lose? He lost

a. his fortune

b. his children

c. his health

d. all the above

D

17. Asaph learned the true secret of life when he

a. read the psalms of David

b. went into the sanctuary

c. saw what happened to Korah

d. lost all his money

D

18. God rewarded Job's patience by

a. having David write a book about him

b. saving his soul

c. giving him double for all he had lost

d. providing him with some friends to comfort him

C

19. James says "swear not." The primary reference is to

a. profanity in general

b. taking an oath in a court of law

c. thoughtlessly using the Lord's or some other name to prove one's honesty

d. using your own name to prove your honesty

A

20. Which of the commandments might James have had in mind when he said "swear not"? The

a. first

b. second

c. third

d. tenth

C

WHAT DO YOU SAY?

To what extent have you learned patience?

_____

_____

_____

_____

_____

Prayer and Healing (James 5:13-15)

The theme of the closing verses of this chapter is prayer. The word occurs seven times, either as a noun or verb.

PRAYER IS ALWAYS APPROPRIATE (5:13)

In every circumstance of life, we should go to the Lord in prayer. When in trouble, we should approach Him with earnest entreaties. In times of rejoicing, we should lift our hearts to Him in praise. He wants to be brought into all the changing moods of our lives.

We should see God as the first great Cause of all that comes to us in life. We should not look into what Rutherford called the "confused rolling of the wheels of second causes." It is defeat to allow ourselves to be victims of circumstances, or to wait for our circumstances to change. We should see no hand but His.

SICKNESS AND PRAYER (5:14-15)

This is one of the most disputed portions of the epistle, and perhaps of the entire New Testament. It brings us face to face with the place of healing in the life of the believer today.

Before looking at the verses in detail, it should be helpful to review what the Bible teaches about sickness and healing.

1. We can agree that all sickness is, in a general way, the result of sin in the world. By this we mean that if sin had never entered, there would be no sickness.

2. Sometimes sickness is a *direct* result of sin in a person's life. In 1 Corinthians 11:30, we read of certain Corinthians who were sick because they participated in the Lord's Supper without judging sin in their lives, that is, without confessing and forsaking it.

3. Not all sickness is a direct result of sin in a person's life. Job was sick in spite of the fact that he was a most righteous man (Job 1:8). The man born blind was not suffering for sins he had committed (John 9:2, 3). Epaphroditus was sick because of his tireless activity in the work of the Lord (Philippians 2:30). Gaius was spiritually healthy but physically unwell (3 John 2).

4. Sometimes sickness is a result of satanic activity. It was Satan who caused Job's body to be covered with boils (Job 2:7). It was Satan who crippled the woman in Luke 13:10-17 so that she was bent double, unable to straighten herself up. Note verse 16, "This woman . . . whom Satan hath bound, lo, these eighteen years. . . ." Paul had a physical infirmity caused by Satan. He called it " . . . a thorn in the flesh, the messenger of Satan to buffet me . . ." (2 Corinthians 12:7).

5. God can and does heal. In a very real sense, all healing is divine. One of the names of God in the Old Testament is *Jehovah-Ropheka*—"Jehovah that healeth thee" (Exodus 15:26). We should acknowledge God in every case of healing.

   It is clear from the Bible that God uses different means in healing. Sometimes He heals through natural bodily processes. He has placed within the human body tremendous powers of recuperation. Sometimes He heals through medicines. Paul advised Timothy, for instance, to use a little wine for his stomach's sake and his often infirmities (1 Timothy 5:23). Sometimes He heals through physicians and surgeons. Jesus explicitly taught that sick people need a physician (Matthew 9:12). Paul spoke of Luke as "the beloved physician" (Colossians 4:14), which certainly recognizes the need of doctors among Christians. God uses doctors in the ministry of healing. As Dubois, the famous French surgeon said, "The surgeon dresses the wound; God heals it."

6. But God also heals miraculously. The Gospels contain many illustrations of this. It would not be correct to say that God generally heals in this way, but neither should we say that He never does. There is nothing in the Bible to discourage us from believing that God can heal miraculously today.

7. Yet we must also be clear that it is not always God's will to heal. Paul left Trophimus sick at Miletum (2 Timothy 4:20). The Lord did not heal Paul of his thorn in the flesh (2 Corinthians 12:7-10). If it were always God's will to heal, some would never grow old or die.

8. God has not promised to heal in every case; therefore, healing is not something we can demand from Him. In Philippians 2:27 healing is spoken of as a mercy, not something which we have a right to expect.

9. While it is true in a general sense that healing is in the "Atonement," yet not all the blessings that are in the Atonement have been given to us yet. For instance, the redemption of the body was included in Christ's work for us, but we will not receive it until Christ comes for His saints (Romans 8:23). At that time also we will be completely and finally healed of all diseases.

10. It is not true that failure to be healed indicates a lack of faith. If it were, this would mean that some would live on indefinitely; but no one does. Paul, Trophimus and Gaius were not healed, and yet their faith was virile and active.

But now we must return to the text of James 5, and see how it fits in with what the rest of the Bible teaches about healing. "Is any sick among you? let him call for the elders of the church; and let them pray over him, anointing him with oil in the name of the Lord: And the prayer of faith shall save the sick, and the Lord shall raise him up; and if he have committed sins, they shall be forgiven him."

If these were the only verses in the Bible on healing, then we would assume that a Christian could be assured of healing from every illness that comes to him in life, if he met the conditions listed. However, we have already seen from other Scriptures that it is not always God's will to heal. Therefore we are forced to the conclusion that James is not talking about *every* kind of illness, but only about a certain form of sickness, that is, a sickness which is the result of certain specific circumstances. The key to understanding the passage is found in the words, " . . . and if he have committed sins, they shall be forgiven him," or as the New English Bible translates it, " . . . and any sins he may have committed will be forgiven." Healing in this section is connected with the forgiveness of sins.

Here is a man who has committed some sin, probably involving the testimony of the local church. Shortly afterward he is stricken with illness. He realizes that this sickness is a direct result of his sin. God is chastening him in order to bring him back into fellowship. He repents of his sin and confesses it to God. But since the sin has also involved the public testimony of the assembly, he calls the elders and makes a full confession to them as well. They pray over him, anointing him with oil in the Name of the Lord. This prayer of faith saves the sick man, and the Lord raises him up. It is a definite promise of the Lord that where sickness is a direct result of sin, and where that sin is confessed and forsaken in the manner described, the Lord will heal.

Someone will say, "How do you know that the man has committed sins and that he is brought to the place of repentance and confession?" The answer is that the closing part of verse 15 speaks about his sins being forgiven. And we know that sins are forgiven only as a result of confession (1 John 1:9).

Someone else will object, "It doesn't say he *has* committed sins. It says *if* he have committed sins." This is true, but the whole context has to do with confession of sins and the restoration of a backslider.

Notice the following—"Confess your faults one to another, and pray one for another, that ye may be healed" (verse 16). The drought mentioned in verses 17 and 18 was a judgment of God on Israel because of sin. It was lifted after they returned to the Lord, acknowledging Him as the true God (1 Kings 18:39). Verses 19 and 20 clearly deal with the recovery of a backslider, as we shall see.

The entire context of James 5:13-20 shows that the healing promised by God is for a person whose sickness is a result of sin, and who confesses the sin to the elders. The responsibility of the elders is to pray over the man, anointing him with oil. Some interpret the oil here as signifying the use of medicinal means, since oil was a form of medicine in the days when James was writing (Luke 10:34). Another view is that the ritual use of oil is meant. This view is strengthened by the words "in the Name of the Lord." In other words, the anointing was to be done by His authority and in obedience to His Word. Oil was sometimes used by the apostles when effecting miraculous cures (Mark 6:13). The healing power was not in the oil, but the oil symbolized the Holy Spirit in His healing ministry (1 Corinthians 12:9).

Some will object that the ritual use of oil is inconsistent with the age of grace, with its de-emphasis on ceremonies and rites. However, we do use the bread and wine as symbols of Christ's body and blood. Also women use head coverings in the assembly as symbols of their subjection to man. Why then should we object to the ritual use of oil?

"The prayer of faith shall save the sick," says James. In response to the prayer of faith, God will heal the person. It is a prayer of faith because it is based on the promise of God's Word. It is not at all a question as to how much faith the elders have, or how much faith the sick man has. The elders can pray with complete assurance because God has promised to raise up the man when the conditions described have been fully met. " . . . And any sins that he has committed will be forgiven." It does not say specifically that the man has committed sins, but it is strongly implied. And it is also implied that the man confesses his sins, since forgiveness is dependent on confession (Proverbs 28:13).

To summarize, then, we believe that verses 14 and 15 apply to a case where a person is sick as a direct result of some sin. When he realizes this and repents, he should call for the elders of the assembly

103

and make a full confession to them. They should then pray over him, anointing him with oil in the Name of the Lord. They can pray for his recovery in faith, since God here promises to heal·the man.

When you have mastered this lesson, take the first part of Exam 6 (covering lesson 11), questions 1-10 on pages 109-110 (right after lesson 12).

Prayer and Restoration (James 5:16-20)

CONFESSION (5:16a)

"Confess your faults one to another, and pray one for another, that ye may be healed." A casual reading of this statement might give the impression that we are to tell other people all about our secret sins. But that is not the thought. Primarily James means that when we sin against someone else, we should be prompt to confess this sin to the person we have wronged.

Also we should pray for one another. Instead of holding grudges and allowing resentments to build up, we should maintain ourselves in fellowship with others through confession and prayer.

Physical healing is linked with spiritual restoration. Notice how James links together confession, prayer and healing. It is a clear intimation of the vital connection between the physical and the spiritual. Man is a tripartite being—spirit, soul and body (1 Thessalonians 5:23). What affects one part of him affects all. In the Old Testament, the priest was also the physician. It was he who diagnosed leprosy, and it was he who pronounced it cured, for instance. By thus combining the offices of priest and doctor in one person, the Lord indicated the close tie between the spirit and the body.

The field of psychosomatic medicine recognizes this link and searches for personal problems that might be causing physical troubles. But modern medicine does not have the remedy for sin. Deliverance from the guilt, defilement, power and penalty of sin can come only on the basis of the blood of Christ, and through confession Godward and manward. More often than we are willing to admit, illnesses are caused by sin—such sins as gluttony, worry, anger, an unforgiving spirit, intemperance, jealousy, selfishness, and pride. Sin in the life brings sickness and sometimes death (1 Corinthians 11:30). We should confess and forsake sin as soon as we are aware it has come into our lives. *All* sin should be confessed to God. In addition, sins against other people should be confessed to them as well. It's vital for our spiritual health and good for our physical health.

HOW ELIJAH PRAYED (5:16b-18)

"Tremendous power is made available through a good man's earnest prayer. Do you remember Elijah? He was a man like us, but he prayed earnestly that it should not rain. In fact, not a drop fell on the land for three and a half years. Then he prayed again; the heavens gave the rain, and the earth sprouted with vegetation as usual" (Phillips). This incident is recorded in 1 Kings 17:1—19:10. Ahab was king of Israel at the time. Through his wife Jezebel, he became a worshipper of Baal, and led the people into this vile form of idolatry. "He did more to provoke the Lord God of Israel to anger than all the kings of Israel that were before him" (16:33). It was as a direct result of sin that drought came upon Israel for three and a half years.

Then Elijah had the notable contest with the priests of Baal on Mt. Carmel. When the fire of the Lord fell and consumed the burnt offering, the altar and the water, the people were convinced and turned back to the Lord. Elijah prayed again and the drought ended. The example of Elijah is given as an encouragement to us to pray for those who have sinned and wandered away from fellowship with God. "The effectual fervent prayer of a righteous man availeth much" (v. 16b) or, as someone has paraphrased it, "The prayer of a man whose heart is right with God works wonders." Lest we be tempted to think of Elijah as belonging to a higher creation than ourselves, James reminds us that he was a man with the same kind of frail flesh (verse 17). He was a mere man, subject to the same weaknesses and infirmities as other men.

PRAYING FOR BACKSLIDERS (5:19, 20)

In the preceding verses we have seen the elders of the assembly being used in the restoration of a sinning saint. And we have seen Elijah being used in the restoration (partial and temporary) of a backsliding nation. Now we are exhorted to give ourselves to this far-reaching ministry.

Verse 19 describes a Christian brother who has wandered away from the truth, either in doctrine or in practice. Another brother makes this a matter of fervent, believing prayer, then lovingly wins him back to fellowship with God and with his brothers and sisters in Christ. How immense is the significance of this ministry! First of all, he saves the erring brother from dying prematurely under the chastening hand of God. Secondly, he covers a multitude of sins. They are forgiven and forgotten by God. Also they are forgiven by fellow-believers and veiled from the gaze of the outside public. We need this ministry today. In our zeal to evangelize the lost, perhaps we do not give sufficient attention to those sheep of Christ who have wandered from the fold.

Once again James has been prodding our consciences with regard to various areas of the Christian life. He has been asking us, for example: Do you lay up treasures on earth? Are your business methods strictly honest? Your income tax return, for instance? Do you live luxuriously, or do you live sacrificially so that others may come to know the Savior? When you sin against another person, are you willing to go to him and apologize? When you become ill, whom do you contact first—the doctor or the Lord? When you see a brother fall into sin, do you criticize him or try to restore him?

CONCLUSION

And so we come to the end of this practical little epistle. In it we have seen faith on trial. We have seen faith tested by the problems of life, by unholy temptations, by obedience to the Word of God. The man who says he has faith has been challenged to exhibit it by avoiding partiality or snobbishness and to prove it by a life of good works. The reality of faith is seen in a person's speech; the believer learns to yield his tongue to the Lordship of Christ. True faith is accompanied by true wisdom; the life of envy and strife is exchanged for that of practical godliness.

Faith avoids the feuds, struggles and jealousies that spring from covetousness and worldly ambition. It avoids a harsh, critical spirit. It avoids the self-confidence which leaves God out of life's plans. Faith stands trial by the way it earns and spends its money. In spite of oppression, it manifests fortitude and endurance in view of the Lord's return. Its speech is uniformly honest, needing no oaths to attest it. Faith goes to God in all the changing moods of life. In sickness, it first looks for spiritual causes. By confession to God and to those who have been wronged, it removes these possible causes. Finally, faith goes out in love and compassion to those who have backslidden.

Your faith and mine are on trial each day. What is the Judge's verdict?

When you are ready, complete Exam 6 by answering questions 11-20 on pages 111-112. (You should have already answered questions 1-10 as part of your study of lesson 11.)

Name_____

Exam
Grade_____

(print plainly)

Address _____

Zip   Class

City_____ State _____ Code _____ Number _____

Instructor _____

LESSON 11

In the blank space in the right-hand margin write the letter of the correct answer.

1. When pressed by adverse circumstances our first reaction should be to
   a. seek to change them
   b. yield to them
   c. see God's hand in them
   d. ignore them if possible

   C

2. 1 Corinthians 11:30 teaches that
   a. all sickness is a direct result of sin
   b. sickness can be a direct result of sin
   c. no sickness is a direct result of sin though it may be an indirect result of sin
   d. no true believer ought ever to be sick

   A B

3. Which of the following suffered physically as a result of Satanic activity?
   a. Epaphroditus
   b. Gaius
   c. The man born blind
   d. Paul

   B

4. Which of the following Old Testament names of God implies that God does heal people?
   a. Jehovah Nissi
   b. Jehovah Ropheka
   c. Jehovah Jireh
   d. Jehovah Shammah

   C

5. Paul told which of the following to take some wine (as medicine) for his upset stomach and other ailments?
a. Timothy
b. Titus
c. Tychicus
d. Trophimus

6. Which of the following proves that it is not always God's will to heal people miraculously?
a. Secundus
b. Barnabas
c. Trophimus
d. Epaphras

7. It is true that healing is in the atonement. This means that
a. no saved person can be sick
b. if we have sufficient faith we will never be sick
c. if we have sufficient faith we will always be healed from sickness
d. at Christ's second coming men will be completely and finally healed of all diseases

8. James, in his passage on healing, is referring to
a. the healing of all men whether saved or not
b. the healing of believers of each and every illness they may have
c. the healing of illness caused by some specific sin involving the testimony of the local church
d. the healing of only those people who go to a faith healer

C

9. The condition of healing, in the case under discussion by James, is
a. sufficient faith in the healer
b. confession of sin to the elders
c. a sufficiently large donation to the church
d. the sickness must be in the mind

B

10. The use of oil in the case mentioned by James is
a. optional
b. medicinal
c. ritualistic
d. psychological

B

WHAT DO YOU SAY?

What is your view of those who set themselves up as "faith healers" and profess to work miraculous cures at mass meetings?

_____

_____

_____

_____

_____

LESSON 12

In the blank space in the right-hand margin write the letter of the correct answer.

11. When James says we should confess our faults one to another he is
    a. advocating public confession of private sins
    b. urging us to publicly confess all our secret sins
    c. telling us to confess our sins to the person we have wronged
    d. speaking primarily to the unsaved
                                    C

12. To confession James links
    a. prayer
    b. good works
    c. penance
    d. death
                                      A

13. Physical healing and spiritual restoration are
    a. divorced by James
    b. linked together by James
    c. only casually associated one with another by James
    d. treated as minor topics by James
                                      B

14. In the Old Testament which of the following also functioned as a physician? The
   a. patriarch
   b. priest
   c. king
   d. judge

   B

15. Which of the following sins can cause sickness?
   a. Anger
   b. Worry
   c. Holding a grudge
   d. All of them

   D

16. *All* sin should be confessed to
   a. a priest
   b. God
   c. the elders
   d. the church

   B

17. For which of the following did Elijah pray? For
   a. drought
   b. rain
   c. both of these
   d. neither of these

   B

18. Elijah was
   a. very unlike us in temperament
   b. a man subject to the same weaknesses as we are
   c. an extraordinary person in that he never gave way to doubt or depression
   d. of a higher order of creation than ordinary people

   B

19. James concludes his epistle by urging us to
   a. evangelize the lost
   b. support faith healers
   c. seek supernatural gifts of the Holy Spirit
   d. pray for erring brethren

   D

20. Pre-eminently, James' epistle is
   a. practical
   b. theological
   c. eschatological
   d. mystical

   A

WHAT DO YOU SAY?

What has helped you most in your study of the epistle of James?

_____

_____

_____

_____

_____

What practical steps have you taken to do what God says?

_____

_____

_____

_____

_____